Lost Ramessid and Post-Ramessid Private Tombs in the Theban Necropolis

CNI PUBLICATIONS 33

LOST RAMESSID AND POST-RAMESSID PRIVATE TOMBS IN THE THEBAN NECROPOLIS

LISE MANNICHE

THE CARSTEN NIEBUHR INSTITUTE OF NEAR EASTERN STUDIES
UNIVERSITY OF COPENHAGEN 2011. MUSEUM TUSCULANUM PRESS

CNI Publications 33
Lost Ramessid and Post-Ramessid Private Tombs in the Theban Necropolis
Museum Tusculanum Press and CNI Publications, 2011
Set in Adobe Garamond Pro by Thora Fisker
Cover design by Thora Fisker
Printed in Denmark by Special-Trykkeriet a-s

ISBN 978 87 635 0534 5
ISSN 0902 5499

This book is published with financial support from
The Carlsberg Foundation
Landsdommer V. Gieses Legat

Published and distributed by
Museum Tusculanum Press
University of Copenhagen
126 Njalsgade
DK-2300 Copenhagen S
Denmark
www.mtp.dk

Contents

Acknowledgements

As it was the case for my earlier study of 18th dynasty tombs in the Theban necropolis, many museums and institutions have answered queries about early travellers and fragments of wall-decoration. I would like in particular to mention the following: The British Library in London for the Hay MSS and the Burton MSS; the Bodleian Library in Oxford for the Wilkinson MSS; the Griffith Institute in Oxford for the Lepsius MSS; and the Faculty of Oriental Studies in Cambridge for access to microfilms of the Hay MSS. Photographs of painted fragments were provided by Ägyptisches Museum in Berlin; the Field Museum in Chicago; Musée du Louvre in Paris; Museo Egizio in Turin; Ny Carlsberg Glyptotek in Copenhagen; and Pelizaeus-Museum in Hildesheim. I am indebted to John R. Harris and Jürgen Osing for assistance in reading 19th-century handwriting and to Geoffrey T. Martin for drawing my attention to certain painted fragments. I owe it to Paul J. Frandsen to have undertaken the final collating of transliterations and translations of the hieroglyphic texts, and to Rune Nyord for his philological comments throughout, especially on the lengthy sections of the Book of the Dead in TT A15. To Elin Rand Nielsen thanks are due for assistance in digital editing of some of the illustrations.

I am grateful to Paul J. Frandsen for accepting my manuscript within the Carsten Niebuhr Publications. The work could not have been carried out without generous grants in 1989 and 2003-4 from the Carlsberg Foundation in Copenhagen, with a subsequent additional grant for covering printing costs. A further contribution for this purpose was received from Landsdommer V. Gieses Legat.

Slangerup, May 2010 — Lise Manniche

Introduction

My interest in Theban tombs goes back to the years between 1969 and 1971 when I was preparing my MA dissertation on ancient Egyptian musical instruments at the University of Copenhagen. In search of unpublished musical scenes I entered a great many tombs some of which were not easily accessible. Later, under the tutelage of J. R. Harris, at that time holding the chair of Egyptology at Copenhagen, we often discussed fragments of painted tombs and in particular those from the tomb of Nebamun, now in the British Museum. Having for a while been intrigued by the 'lost' tombs with A, B, C and D numbers in the Appendix to the *Topographical Bibliography* I,1, my interest in early travellers was awakened, and for the purposes of my PhD dissertation at the University of Cambridge I decided to attempt a reconstruction on paper of the 18th-dynasty 'lost' tombs. This work was published in 1988 as *Lost Tombs. A Study of Eighteenth Dynasty Monuments in the Theban Necropolis.* During the course of the work on the records of the early travellers, notably those of R. Hay, I also collected material pertaining to the later Theban tombs. I was able to pursue this task in the years 1989-90, but then had to abandon it due to other commitments. In 2003, thanks to a generous grant from the Carlsberg Foundation who had previously supported my studies in this field, I was finally able to take up my research once more and bring it to completion, the text being revised, digitalised, and updated and the illustrations checked and improved for publication.

As the work has been extended over a long period during which progress in computer technology has exploded, this has involved a certain amount of reworking of my original artwork which was based primarily on copying Hay's facsimile tracings. These were made on semi-opaque sheets of tracing paper, now yellow, in faint pencil line. The technique used by Hay's artists was to copy thick contours as thin, double lines. This is not how Hay would have wanted it published, nor would most modern draughtsmen. Hence it was in the 1980s decided to re-draw and fill in such double lines in ink. These large drawings have now been scanned and reduced in size. Some of them, however, have been further edited on the computer screen, notably the lengthy section of the Book of the Dead in TT A16 where it was ultimately decided to remove all traces of dividing lines, which had been applied at random by Hay's artists. If the task had been tackled from scratch after the digital revolution, a different method might have been chosen, but such were the conditions at the time. The method of reproduction is explicitly stated in relation to each figure reproduced in this work.

A number of studies which have appeared in recent years have facilitated the hypothetical reconstruction of the scheme of decoration of tombs that are no longer extant, in particular the extensive two volume publication by Friederike Kampp from 1996 on the architecture of all the private tombs in the area,[1] and the study by Petra Barthelmess on funerary rites in Ramessid tombs from 1992 with a useful table of positions of the individual scenes in known tombs.[2] This confirms what can be read from isolated scenes based on the subject and its orientation as practised in the author's publication of 18th-dynasty lost tombs and during the earlier stages of work on the present volume.

1 *Die thebanische Nekropole* I-II.
2 *Die Übergang ins Jenseits in den thebanischen Beamtengräbern der Ramessidenzeit.*

Early travellers

The subject of early travellers[3] has been studied in some detail in recent years. Those mentioned in the present work are the following (in the approximate order in which they first appear at Thebes):

Piccinini, who was active in the necropolis from around 1820-30, is the most shadowy figure although he is frequently mentioned. He was obviously of Italian extraction (his first name remains unknown). Although he was chiefly in the employment of B. Drovetti, as a man with local knowledge he was much in demand by many other foreigners who stayed for a longer or shorter period in the area. His house was in the northern part of the necropolis (see below), many of the lost tombs with A numbers being located with reference to it. This would be the area he knew best and explored most extensively.

Yanni (1799-1854),[4] whose full name was Giovanni d'Athanasi, was Piccinini's colleague in the employment of Henry Salt. He is the author of a booklet on his discoveries at Thebes (*Researches and discoveries in Upper Egypt made under the direction of Henry Salt Esq.* (1836)), and he also appears frequently in the notes and diaries of travellers in the 1820s. His headquarters were in a large house at the foot of Sheikh Abd el-Qurna (see below).

John Gardner Wilkinson (1797-1875) is the one among the early travellers who spent the longest uninterrupted period in the necropolis (1821-33). He, too, resided at Sheikh Abd el-Qurna (see below). He made tracings and a vast amount of sketches which were published in 1837, and later reprinted many times, in his *Manners and Customs of the Ancient Egyptians.*[5] His manuscripts are in the Bodleian Library, Oxford.

Robert Hay (1799-1863) distinguished himself by collecting a team of artists who during several longer stays in the necropolis made excellent tracings of a substantial amount of tomb reliefs and paintings. Combined with Hay's own camera lucida drawings, often enhanced in watercolour, and careful descriptions they form an invaluable source for monuments now destroyed or lost. Regrettably, all he ever published were his drawings of Cairo.[6] His manuscripts are in the British Library. Hay mostly resided in Wilkinson's house.

Joseph Bonomi (1796-1878) spent time as draughtsman in the employment of Hay and others for eight years from 1824 and later joined the expedition of Lepsius. He had a hand in a great variety of publications on Ancient Egypt.

A. Dupuy was a French artist who worked with Bonomi and Hay.

James Burton (1788-1862) was an independent traveller who pursued his own interests, and apart from a huge amount of plans and other drawings he recorded scenes of wall-decoration in his notebooks. In 1824 he joined Hay and Wilkinson at Thebes and came back once more in the 1830s. He left a large collection of records, now in the British Library.

3 Cf. W. R. Dawson and E. Uphill, *Who was who in Egyptology*, 1995.
4 Yanni's death certificate has recently been discovered by John Taylor, see R. B. Parkinson, *Reading Ancient Egyptian Poetry*, 2009, p. 225.
5 For a biography of Wilkinson see J. Thompson, *Sir Gardner Wilkinson and his Circle*, 1992.
6 For a biography of Hay see S. Tillet, *Egypt Itself*, 1984.

Jean François Champollion (1790-1832). His work was published posthumously as *Monuments de l'Égypte et de la Nubie* I-IV 1835-47. For the present purposes Champollion's work went in tandem with that of

Ippolito Rosellini (1800-1843). To a large extent the two scholars copied and published the same scenes in their respective splendid works in French and Italian. Occasionally, however, there are differences and a close study of both needs to be carried out. The results of Rosellini's work were published as *I monumenti dell'Egitto e della Nubia* I-III 1832-44. His unpublished MSS are kept in Pisa.

Karl Richard Lepsius (1810-1884) is the most recent of those who come into the group of 'early travellers'. His Prussian expedition took place in 1842-45, resulting in the mammoth publication *Denkmäler aus Aegypten und Aethiopien* I-XII (1849-59). His notebook with unpublished material is now kept in Berlin, having previously spent a long time on loan to the Griffith Institute in Oxford.

Notes on the topography of the Theban necropolis

Failing a detailed map of the private tombs of the Theban necropolis one must rely on sketched or earlier maps.[7] Among the former are the reference maps reproduced in sections in the *Topographical Bibliography* in 1960/1970[8] with all tomb numbers, but few topographical details, and the useful separate, overall map published by the German Archaeological Institute in the 1970s.[9] Maps from the days of the early travellers themselves include the large map drawn by Wilkinson and published as *Topography of Thebes* from 1835 and a map in colour drawn by F. Catherwood (1799-1855) for Robert Hay, now Hay MSS 28816,1, partly reproduced in black and white in D. Eigner fig. 4.[10] Notes collected by Bonomi were appended to the map in the Hay MSS and later published by Newberry in *ASAE* 7, 1906, pp. 78-86.

For the present work a xerox copy[11] of the map of Wilkinson was used as a basis for adding some important points of reference encountered in connection with the whereabouts of the lost tombs. For practical reasons sections of the German map are reproduced here covering Draᶜ abu el-Nagaᶜ (concerning tombs with A-numbers, north of the Deir el-Bahari causeway) and Sheikh ᶜabd el-Qurna, Khokha and Assasif (concerning tombs with B and C numbers, south of the Deir el-Bahari causeway). Even more useful than the maps because of the rendering of hilly and uneven ground are the photographs published in A. H. Gardiner and A. E. P. Weigall's *Topography of Thebes* of 1913 with tomb numbers inserted, especially pl. XI (Draᶜ abu el-Nagaᶜ) and pl. III (Sheikh ᶜabd el-Qurna).

7 For an aerial view of the entire necropolis, commissioned by the Theban Mapping Project in 1979, see www.thebanmappingproject.com /Atlas of the Theban Necropolis

8 B. Porter and R. L. B. Moss, *Topographical Bibliography of Ancient Egyptian Hieroglyphic Texts, Reliefs, and Paintings*, I,1.

9 No details of publication are included on the map.

10 D. Eigner, *Die monumentalen Grabbauten der Spätzeit in der thebanischen Nekropole,* 1984.

11 Kindly provided by the Griffith Institute.

1
4
5
6
7
8
A
B
C
D
T
U
I
J
A1
B1
C1
D1
801-10
1101-3
1156-61
2001-5

German map showing the location of known and numbered tombs. The presumed location of 'lost' tombs is as follows: A-numbers "10", B-numbers "8" and "9" and C-numbers "7".

The following reference points are particularly relevant:

Dra῾ abu el-Naga῾:

Deir el-Bakhit. The ruined Coptic monastery high up on the main hill of the southern part of Dra῾ abu el-Naga῾. The hill itself was known as Shiq el-Atiyat. The monastery is now being explored by the German institute.[12]

El-Mandara. On Wilkinson's map this name is given to two ruined brick pyramids at Dra῾ abu el-Naga῾. The one referred to in relation to the lost tombs appears to be the one numbered Q which must be 'the brick pyramid of Piccinini'.

Piccinini's house. This was located near TT 161 at Dra῾ abu el-Naga῾. It was actually drawn by Nestor l'Hôte who joined Champollion's expedition as a draughtsman.[13]

On Wilkinson's map, the letters C, D, E, G, J, L, R, S, T, V, W, Y, Y2 all refer to 'painted' tombs, not all of which are 'lost tombs'.

Sheikh ῾abd el-Qurna:

Wilkinson's house was inside TT 83 half way up the hill. It appears in a number of contemporary drawings.[14]

Yanni's house was further down towards the plain. Until the total demolition of the houses in the area, begun in 2006, the ruins had survived.[15]

A. Dupuy resided in TT 65 of Imiseba,[16] then known as Bab el-Gaafa.

Assasif:

The house of F. Caillaud, then known as Dêr Sekaio ('the monastery of monsieur Caillaud'), was a large brick building at the entrance to the Assasif, no. 12 on Catherwood's map. Caillaud visited Egypt as early as in 1815 and returned in 1819 and 1821.

El-Birabe ('ruins of a temple'), a name applied to Bab el-Goria, a tomb where Yanni found a variety of objects. (Also used for the storerooms of the Ramesseum and for the low walls in front of Piccinini's house at Dra῾ abu el-Naga῾).

12 G. Burkardt *et al.*, 'Die spätantike-koptische Klosteranlage Deir el-Bachit' (1), 2003, pp. 41-65; I. Eichner and U. Fauerbach, 'Die spätantike/koptische Klosteranlage Deir el-Bachit in Dra῾ Abu el-Naga῾ (Oberägypten). Zweiter Vorbericht', 2005, pp. 139-152.

13 Published by C. Simpson in N. Strudwick & J. H. Taylor (eds.), *The Theban Necropolis*, fig. 1 p. 248. See also J. Thompson, *Sir Gardner Wilkinson and his Circle* 1992, p. 105.

14 J. Thompson, *Sir Gardner Wilkinson and his Circle*, pp. 101ff. The house is visible in the distance in C. Simpson in N. Strudwick & J. H. Taylor (eds.), *The Theban Necropolis*, p. 247, ill. 145 (from the 1862 publication by A. H. Rhind).

15 See C. Simpson in N. Strudwick & J. H. Taylor (eds.), *The Theban Necropolis*, p. 247, ill. 146 (photo 1998) and ill. 145 (from the 1862 publication by A. H. Rhind).

16 See T. A. Bács, 'First preliminary report on the work of the Hungarian mission in Thebes in Theban Tomb No. 65 (Nebamun/Imiseba)', 1998, pp. 49-64 with reference to Dupuy on pp. 53-4.

Part I Ramessid Tombs

TT A12

This monument was situated at Draᶜ abu el-Nagaᶜ, below the ruins of the monastery of Deir el-Bakhit.[17] Wilkinson called it 'the tomb of the hill of the brick pyramid of Piccinini'.[18] Champollion gave the tomb the number 40, whereas in the Rosellini MSS it is down as no. 41. It should be mentioned that TT 157 of Nebwcncncf, a namesake of our tomb-owner, was Champollion's tomb no. 42, and one may perhaps take it that because of its numbering, it was not too distant from our tomb, his no. 40.[19] TT 157 is located above TT 161.

The tomb is mentioned in the following works, cf. *Top. Bibl.* I,1, p. 451: Wilkinson MSS v.208; Rosellini MSS 284, G54; Champollion, *Not. descr.* i, p. 534.

The owner of the tomb and its date

In the previous century, the name and title of the tomb-owner had survived in at least one scene. He was *imy-r sẖty n pr imn nbwnnf* 'overseer of the peasants in the estate of Amun, Nebwenenef'. The title recurs in an offering scene where the name is no longer extant. In another instance the same title is followed by a different name, Mahu. Another title copied in the tomb by Wilkinson was *ḥm(t?) nṯr n ḥwtḥr* 'prophet(ess?) of Hathor'.

Judging from the name of the tomb-owner and the choice of scenes on the walls, a Ramessid date would be appropriate for this tomb.

The decoration of the tomb

Only Wilkinson made sketches of the decoration of this tomb, and only of two of the scenes, but all three early travellers copied some of the inscriptions. According to Champollion, the tomb would appear to have had more than one room, the 'first one' being decorated with 'paintings of a surprising freshness, but mediocre style'. Rosellini refers to it as 'a small painted tomb', adding that the names of the deceased had been erased ('cancellati'). But this was evidently only true in some cases.

The following subjects were depicted:

Scene A. Tomb-owner offering to Amenhotpe I and queen Ahmosi Nefertere
Scene B. Tomb-owner offering to Osiris and Ra
Scene C. Hathor cow in the mountain
Scene D. Priest offering to tomb-owner and wife
Scene E. A colleague of the tomb-owner

17 Deir el-Bakhit is N on Wilkinson's map (for a sketch by Wilkinson of the ruined building see N. Strudwick & J. H. Taylor (eds.), *The Theban Necropolis*, ill. 139). M is 'Bab el-Masikh' which may be = TT 158 (see P. E. Newberry, 'Topographical notes on Western Thebes collected in 1830 by Joseph Bonomi', 1906, p. 84 (67). Cf. Kampp, *Die thebanische Nekropole*, p. 116: near TT 157?

18 On Wilkinson's map, a pyramid is indicated south of the area where TT 161 is located.

19 *Sic* also Kampp, *Die thebanische Nekropole,* p. 116.

Scene A
Tomb-owner offering to Amenhotpe I and queen Ahmosi Nefertere[20]

Text: Wilkinson MSS v.208 [upper right and middle]; Rosellini MSS 284, G54 (part); Champollion, *Not. descr.* i, p. 534.
This scene was mentioned by all three early travellers, who made identical copies of the royal names. These are Rosellini's and Wilkinson's versions:

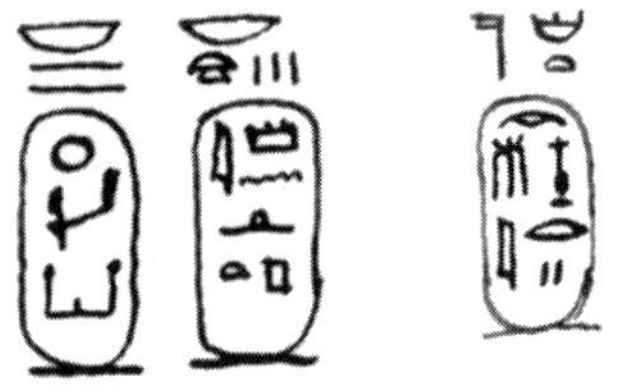

Fig. 1 Rosellini MSS 284, G54

Fig. 2 TT A12 Wilkinson MSS v.208 [upper right]

nb tꜣwy ḏsrkꜣrꜥ nb ḫꜥw ỉmnḥtp ḥmt nṯr ỉꜣḥms nfrtỉrỉ

'Lord of the Two Lands, Djeserkara, son of Ra, lord of crowns/appearances Amenhotpe, god's wife Ahmosi Nefertere.'

All early travellers agree that the complexion of the queen was black, the king having the conventional red body colour.[21]
Wilkinson also copied the inscription pertaining to the tomb-owner adoring the royal couple:

Fig. 3 Willkinson MSS v.208 [middle]

ỉꜣw n kꜣ.k ḏsrkꜣrꜥ sꜣ rꜥ ỉmnḥtp sn tꜣ n ḥmt nṯr ỉꜥḥms nfrtỉrỉ
ỉn wsỉr ỉmy-r[22] *sḫty n pr ỉmn nbwnnf mꜣꜥ ḫrw nb...*

'Praise to your *ka*, Djeserkara, son of Ra, Amenhotpe; kissing the ground to the god's wife Ahmosi Nefertere by Osiris, overseer of the peasants of the estate of Amun, Nebwenenef, justified, lord of(?)...'

The concluding *nb* could be either the beginning of the inscription pertaining to the tomb-owner's wife, but with the affiliation omitted; or, more likely, it could be read as *[ḫr] nb [ḏt]* 'with the lord of eternity', the preposition being omitted.
The royal couple would be seated facing left, with the tomb-owner, perhaps joined by his wife, facing right, i.e. in the same direction as the hieroglyphs describing the act they perform. One would expect them to stand opposite the deified royal couple. Above his copy of the hieroglyphs Wilkinson scribbled 'man praying to king and queen *above*', but this no doubt refers to his copy of the cartouches on top of the *page.*

20 For similar representations in other Ramessid tombs one may compare the following (omitting Deir el-Medina). Numbers refer to tombs and scenes as quoted in the *Top. Bibl.*I,1: 16 (6); 23 (24); 44 (5); 554 (5); 106 (D); 113 (2) (now in the British Museum); 141 (6); 149 (6); 178 (2); 285 (19); 300 (6); 302 (3); 306 (2) – (4); 344 (7); 375 (1). Further discussion and bibliography of the posthumous representations of Amenhotpe I will be found under TT A18 below.
21 For a discussion by the author on the complexion of this queen, see 'The complexion of queen Ahmosi Nefertari', 1979, pp. 11-19.
22 Wilkinson copied the viper *f* for the tongue.

Scene B
Tomb-owner offering to Osiris and to Ra

Champollion, *Not. descr.* i, p. 534.

Little can be said about this scene except for the mere fact that it had a place in our tomb. It was briefly mentioned by Champollion: (tomb-owner) 'faisant diverses offrandes et adorations à Osiris, à Phré et au couple royal…', but reference to the subject was omitted in the *Top. Bibl.* From the way in which Champollion phrased it, we may perhaps imply that the two scenes were juxtaposed. Osiris and Ra are usually seated under separate canopies.

Scene C
Hathor cow in mountain

Wilkinson MSS v.208 [upper right].

This subject was sketched in ink by Wilkinson with the caption 'cow coming out of the hill of Hathor'. The cow with the usual disc, feathers and menat necklace emerges from the mountainside on the right. Hence it was presumably positioned at the right extremity of a left wall, with its back towards the West.

Fig. 4 Wilkinson MSS v.208 [upper right]

Scene D
Priest offering to tomb-owner and wife

Wilkinson MSS v.208 [lower].

Fig. 5 Wilkinson MSS v.208 [lower]

Part of this scene was sketched in ink by Wilkinson (MSS v.208 [lower]). It shows the hands of a priest, facing left, with a vase and an incense burner in front of a large bundle of onions on a table. The couple would have been seated on the other side of the vegetables, facing right. The inscriptions run as follows:

irt sntr [ḳ]bḥ n wsir imy-r sḫty...
n kꜣ n wsir imy-r sḫty pr imn ḥsy...

'Performing (the act of giving) incense and cool water to Osiris, overseer of peasants... – To the ka of Osiris, overseer of peasants of the estate of Amun, praised...'

To the left of the copy of this inscription, with the legend 'also', Wilkinson added the title of [hieroglyphs] *ḥm(t?) nṯr n ḥwtḥr* 'prophet(ess?) of Hathor' – possibly the title of the tomb-owner's wife.
Elaborate bell-shaped bundles of onions are not unusual in the scheme of wall-decoration of Ramessid tombs, symbolising the resurrection of the deceased with reference to the life cycle of Osiris-Sokar.[23]

Scene E
Offering to Anubis

Wilkinson saw the following inscription next to a man (facing right) at an offering table (MSS v.208 [middle]):

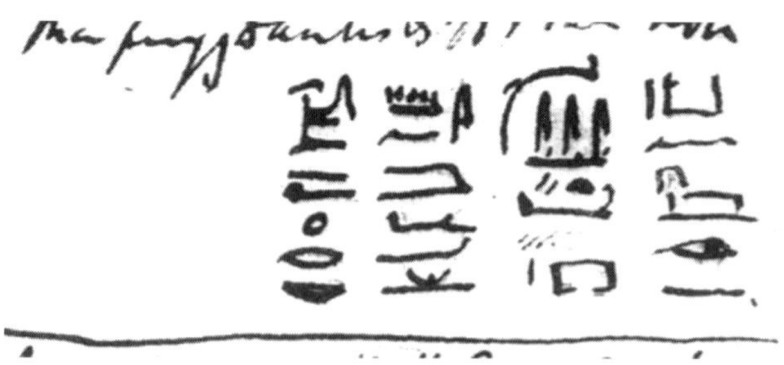

Fig. 6 Wilkinson MSS v.208 [middle upper]

[n] k3 n wsỉr n(?) ỉmy-r sḫty pr ỉmn mꜥḥw m3ꜥ ḫrw ḫr nb...

'[To] the ka of Osiris, to the overseer of the peasants of the estate of Amun, Mahu, justified under the lord...'

Wilkinson added the following caption: 'Man praying to Anubis & offerings on a table'. The man would be facing right and Anubis left. There appears to be a discrepancy regarding the recipient: is this Anubis, or is it Mahu? He must have been a relative of Nebwenenef who shared his occupation, perhaps a son or his father? But since, according to Rosellini, some names in the tomb were erased, it is also possible that Mahu is the name of either the original owner or the usurper. The hieroglyphs suggest that he was shown being offered to, not in the course of adoring any of the deities recorded in the tomb, hence the scene was presumably in a lower register on the right wall.

Possible position of the recorded scenes

The five subjects mentioned above should all be located on the four walls of one room of a small tomb, each of the walls being probably divided into two registers. Part of the space would have been taken up by the entrance door and (probably) by an entrance to another room, cf. Champollion's description of the tomb as being a 'petite tombe dont la 1ère chambre...'. When Wilkinson recorded the tomb, he drew a horizontal line under each section, except in the case of the scene with the royal couple and that of the Hathor cow (scenes A

23 *e.g.* TT 51, 296, 341. See C. Graindorge, 'Les oignons de Sokar', 1982, pp. 87-105 (omitting reference to our tomb).

and C). Both would face in the same direction (i.e. left) and thus probably belong on a left wall, perhaps (due to the missing dividing line) in the same register. The cow would probably be at the inner part of the wall. Adoration of Osiris and Ra (scene B of which we ignore the orientation) could possibly be fitted in on the right wall. Scene D, priest offering to couple, would belong on the right wall with the couple facing the outside world in a lower register as was often the case in Ramessid tombs and stelae.[24] Judging from the direction of the hieroglyphs, the remaining scene featuring Mahu in a receiving role should also be in this register.

TT A14

Little is known about this tomb, mention of which was only made by Hay in his notebook. He said that it had a brick-walled court, and that it had traces of good sculpture. As he mentions 'the 1st chamber', we must take it that the tomb had more than one room. It was apparently located behind Piccinini's house[25] and hence close to TT A12. Being provided with a court, the tomb must be on the part of the slope that offered such space. The tomb had sculpted decoration. Only one scene was sketched, but it would have been of considerable interest:

Scene A
King in window

Hay MSS 29824, 5 verso [lower].

On the right side of the rear wall of the first room there was a representation of a king leaning on a cushion in a window of appearances and speaking 'as at Medinet Habu' (*sic!*). Hay[26] compared it to the similar scene in TT 157.[27] In front of the sovereign in question were two cartouches (here sketched by the author from the Hay MSS):

Fig. 7 LM sketch from Hay MSS 29824, 5 verso [lower]

The one on the left (to be read as the second cartouche) with its *ḥtpḥrmꜣʿt* element is reminiscent of the prenomen of Merenptah,[28] except that the *n* after *mr* is absent in Hay's copy. The one on the right, as copied by Hay with the *stp-n-Rʿ*-element otherwise chosen by several kings of the 19th dynasty, is not attested for Merenptah, whose first cartouche would have contained *Baenra-Meriamun*. Perhaps the ancient scribe made a mistake, carried out by the sculptor, or Hay mistook the ram for the *stp*-sign. Both these suggestions are

24 Cf. n. 41 below (TT A 15).

25 *Sic Top. Bibl.* I,1, p. 451.

26 MSS 29824,8: 'In a large tomb (sc. TT 157) much destroyed a little to the north are these [drawing of the cartouches of Ramesses II and queen Nefertere]. He leans on a cushion as in a case before mentioned' (sc. TT A 14 on p. 5 verso).

27 For TT 157 see L. Borchardt, 'Die Königin bei einer feierlichen Staatshandlung Ramses' II', 1931, pls. I, II; K. Sethe, 'Die Berufung eines Hohenpriesters des Amon unter Ramses II', 1907-8, pp. 30-5 (text of owner's installation as High Priest of Amun in year 1 of Ramesses II); U. Hölscher, *The Excavation of Medinet Habu*, iii, 1941, fig. 22, p. 44; L. Bell, 'Return to Draʿ Abu el Nagaʿ, 1969, ill. p. 32 [upper].

28 As copied, for example, in TT 23, see Lepsius, *Text* iii, p. 252.

most unsatisfactory, but it is highly unlikely that in this context the cartouche could read anything but Baenra. Merenptah occurs with his father, Ramesses II, twice: once in a statue group with two kings and Osiris,[29] and another time on a stela where the two double cartouches are juxtaposed.[30]

The rest of the scene was destroyed. Judging from the direction of the hieroglyphs and the position of the scene on the right rear wall, the sovereign must have been shown facing right with the tomb-owner and attendants standing in front of him, facing left. The king would thus have had his back to a doorway leading further into the tomb in the manner of kings in many 18th dynasty tombs.

One other Theban tomb depicts Merenptah in action through or in front of his palace window. In TT 23 at Sheikh ʿabd el-Qurna there is a scene showing the tomb-owner being rewarded before Merenptah.[31]

Two of the relevant scenes in Theban tombs from TT 106 (Sethi I) and 157 (Ramesses II) respectively have conveniently been put together by Abdel-Qader Muhammed.[32] A third in TT 217, now largely destroyed, was drawn by Nina de G. Davies.[33] Both have sculpted decoration. TT 106 at Sheikh ʿabd el-Qurna shows the tomb-owner being anointed and hung with golden necklaces. The figure of the king, facing right, is largely destroyed, but he was seated inside a building supported by slender columns, and a window is not shown. TT 157 (which was apparently not too distant from our tomb) concerns not rewarding as such, but the installation of the tomb-owner as vizier in the first year of Ramesses II. The king is depicted inside the palace, leaning towards a window and facing left on a cushion, extending his hand to his subordinate. Apart from the orientation of the scene, this we must take as being the closest parallel to the one in TT A14 as Hay himself made reference to it. The scene from TT 23 being unpublished apart from the texts, there remains only the one from TT 50 (reign of Haremhab) of a comparable date to be mentioned. This latter was copied by Hay.[34] Here the king stands on the ground, level with the tomb-owner, with the window behind him. In this context, one may also consider the sculpted representation, now in the Louvre, from the tomb of Hormin at Saqqara (reign of Sethi I)[35] showing the tomb-owner with ointment and necklaces. Due to the opportunity of depicting the king, rewarding scenes were popular in the Amarna Period, but the motif as such goes back to the reign of Tuthmosis III.[36] In the 18th dynasty, the preferred position (though not the only one) in the wall-decoration for this subject was on either side of the doorway leading to the inner room(s). In the Ramessid tombs it still belonged in the entrance hall but it had moved to the front walls of the hall with the king having his back to the entrance door, whether he faces right (TT 106, also TT 23?) or left (TT 157). TT 217 at Deir el-Medina is the exception among the three, for the king is turned towards the entrance. As the artist in our tomb would have had the scene in TT 157 at close hand, we may perhaps deduce that he placed his motif on the opposite wall (left front wall) in order not to make a too obvious duplicate

If the closest parallel to the scene in TT A14 was indeed the one in TT 157, that is to say an installation scene, the tomb-owner may be none other than the new vizier. Like those of his predecessors, the mortuary temple of the Merenptah at Thebes was provided with a ceremonial palace. In recent years the complex has been excavated and restored by the Swiss Institute in Cairo, but remains of the palace are scarce.[37]

29 Cairo CGC 1208, see K*RI* IV,102.

30 Cairo JdE 28961, see K*RI* IV, 150.

31 Unpublished except for complete text K*RI*, IV, 111-2 and cartouches in *LD Text* iii, p. 252.

32 *The Development of the Funerary Beliefs and Practises in the Private Tombs of the New Kingdom at Thebes*, 1966, pls. 21 and 22.

33 N. de G. Davies, *Two Ramesside Tombs at Thebes*, 1927, pl. XXVII.

34 Camera lucida drawing with some colours added in MSS 29844 A, 194, reproduced in L. Manniche, *City of the Dead,* fig. 50.

35 C 213 (E 3337): C. Boreux, *Guide-Catalogue sommaire,* 1932, i, pl. viii (with king omitted: C. Ziegler, *Le Louvre. Les antiquités égyptiennes,* 1990/1993, p. 48).

36 See A. Radwan, *Darstellungen des regierenden Königs in den Beamtengräbern der 18. Dynastie*, 1969.

37 H. Jaritz *et al.* , 'Der Totentempel des Merenptah', 1992-2001.

On either side of the chamber were two rock-cut seated statues, both couples being 'quite defaced'. In the group 'at the north end', only the woman remained with a smaller figure standing by her left leg. F. Kampp has suggested that our tomb may be = TT 157 belonging to Newenenef, first prophet of Amun.[38] As mentioned above, this tomb was also known by the early travellers, including Hay, but as he makes a *comparison* with the scene in TT 157 (described on his p. 8), it obviously cannot be the same tomb as the one he was describing (on p. 5 verso). As mentioned above, the king in our tomb also faces right whereas the king in TT 157 faces left.

The owner of the tomb

The name of the tomb-owner was not recorded. In view of the presence of the sovereign in a window of appearances, he must have been of a certain standing and been either appointed or rewarded by the sovereign. The officials of the reign of Merneptah have been listed by Kitchen.[39] Among those whose occupation would merit inclusion of a scene depicting the king, and who are known to have had some connection with the Theban area, are the three whose Theban tombs are known: Tjay, chief of the treasury and royal letter-writter (TT 23, including rewarding scene mentioned above); Amenwahsu, first prophet of Monthu (TT 274); and Roma/Roy, high priest of Amun (TT 283). The latter two are by Kitchen assumed to have held their office in the reign of Merneptah. No tomb of a vizier of this time has been identified in spite of the fact that we are familiar from a variety of sources[40] with the person holding that position under Merneptah: Panehsy. The only Panehsy in the Theban necropolis is the prophet of 'Amenophis of the Forecourt' of TT 16 (temp. Ramesses II). Perhaps TT A14 was the tomb of his namesake in the following reign?

For this tomb the *Top. Bibl.* suggests a date around Ramesses II(?), identifying the king in the window as this one. But in view of the presence of the cartouche of his successor, this date should now be modified.

38 Kampp, *Die thebanische Nekropole*, p. 616 without argumentation.
39 K*RI* IV,15, index pp. vii-x.
40 K*RI* IV, 83-93.

Fig. 8 Hay MSS 29851, 89-98 (re-drawn by LM)

TT A15

This tomb was no. 39 of Champollion, no. 40 of Rosellini, situated, like the previous ones, at Draʿ abu el-Nagaʿ 'near Piccinini's house' (Hay MSS 29852, before folio 89); 'a little beyond Piccinini's' (Wilkinson MSS v.111); 'dopo la casa' (Rosellini MSS 284, G53). This was by the *Top. Bibl.* I,1, p. 451 interpreted as 'a little north of Piccinini's house'.

Wilkinson copied scenes on two walls and the texts of a further subject. Hay made excellent tracings of one register. Champollion only copied a few texts, while Rosellini restricted himself to making notes of the names and titles of the tomb-owner and his wife. For a full bibliography see under the individual scenes below.

The owner of the tomb

Our tomb-owner was called by the name of [hieroglyphs] Amenemib. He held the office of [hieroglyphs] *ḥri iryw-ʿ3 n pr imn* 'head of door-keepers in the estate of Amun'. His wife was [hieroglyphs] Irtiʿat, a [hieroglyphs] *šmʿyt n imn n mwt* 'songstress of Amun and of Mut'.

The decoration of the tomb and its date

The tomb had just one little room, reflecting the presumably rather modest status of a head door-keeper, the walls to the 'right' and 'left' being decorated, although according to Champollion the remaining walls had also been prepared for painting. The subjects in the lower register on the 'right' never got beyond the initial outline drawing. Part of the painted stucco of the entrance had come off, but the scene on the (upper) 'right' wall was 'd'une admirable fraicheur'. This was the weighing and conducting scene, published by Wilkinson and also skilfully traced by Hay's team of artists. Rosellini called it 'a tiny little room where only the two side walls are painted.'

Fig. 9 Wilkinson MSS v.211 [upper] (extreme right now obscured)

The tomb has the appearance of a Ramessid tomb. F. Kampp suggests 20th dynasty or later without further argumentation.[41] Although this would not be entirely out of the question, there are no compelling reasons why it should be later than the 20th dynasty.

Left wall[42]
Upper register

Wilkinson, *Manners and Customs*, 2 Ser. Supp. pl. 88 = ed. Birch, iii, pl. lxxi, facing p. 464. Two figures on left reproduced in C. Seeber, *Totengericht,* fig. 27.
Wilkinson MSS v.211 [upper]; Hay MSS 29851, 89-98.
Texts: Champollion, *Not. descr.*, i, p. 850-1; text of Ammet: Rosellini MSS 284, G53 [lower].

Scene A
Weighing scene

The register is surmounted by a polychrome border, and it shows two episodes of the judgment of the deceased, Spells 30B and 125 of the Book of the Dead. To the left the deceased couple is witnessing the crucial ceremony of the weighing of the heart against a figurine of Maat. Anubis adjusts the scales which are decorated with the feather of Maat; Thoth records the proceedings; and Ammet, the monster, awaits the outcome sitting on top of a small shrine. The text above Horus and the couple is as follows:

←

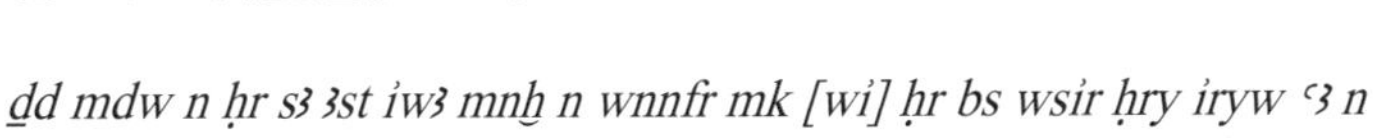

ḏd mdw n ḥr sꜣ ꜣst iwꜣ mnḫ n wnnfr mk [wi] ḥr bs wsir ḥry iryw ꜥꜣ n imn imnmib mꜣꜥ ḫrw ii ḫr.k. nb imntt wsir ḥkꜣ ꜥnḫw iw irtin.k mꜣꜥt r nb twi rḫ.k[wi] ꜥnḫ.k im.s n kꜣ n wsir ḥry iryw ꜥꜣ imnmib snt.f nbt pr ir(t)yꜥꜣt mꜣꜥ[t ḫrw]

41 Kampp, *Die thebanische Nekropole*, p. 617.

42 Sic Rosellini ('a sinistra'). Champollion has right wall ('paroi de droite'), followed by *Top. Bibl.*, but see further below. Due to the direction of the figures, the scene would be placed on a wall to the left, Osiris having his back to the mountain, corresponding to the deceased couple entering from the right on the opposite wall.

'Words to be recited by Horus, son of Isis, splendid heir of Wennufer: Look, [I] introduce Osiris, head door-keeper of Amun, Amenemib, justified. I have come to you, O lord of the West, Osiris, ruler of the living. I have done maat for you every day. I know what you live on. To the ka of Osiris, head door-keeper Amenemib (and) his wife, mistress of the house, Ir(t)y'at, justified.'[43]

Above Anubis:

→

ḏd mdw in inpw ḥry sštꜣ imy wt mk[.wi] ḥr sip imnmib ḥr-ꜥ mḫꜣt[44] *m st.f*

'Words to be recited by Anubis, chief of secrets, who is in the embalming house: Look, I inspect Amenemib on the scales in[45] his/its place.'

Above Thoth:

→

ḏd mdw in ḏḥwty nb mdt ntr wpw mꜣꜥ n psḏt nṯrw mk [.wi] ḥr sš rn ḥry-[iryw]ꜥꜣ imnmib iw ib.f prt ḥr mḫꜣt bw gm[46]*(tw) n.f sp sn ḫr.f*

'Words to be recited by Thoth, lord of divine words, true messenger of the Ennead: Look, I write down the name of the chief door-keeper Amenemib. His heart comes forth on the scales without a second fault being found with him.'

Above Ammet:

→

Scene B
Conducting the tomb-owner to Osiris

The episode on the right, juxtaposed with the previous one, features Amenemib, this time without his wife (she did not fail the ordeal, for we meet her later), being introduced by Horus to Osiris, sitting in his booth with Isis and Nephthys standing behind his throne, and with the four sons of Horus perched on a lotus flower next to him.

←
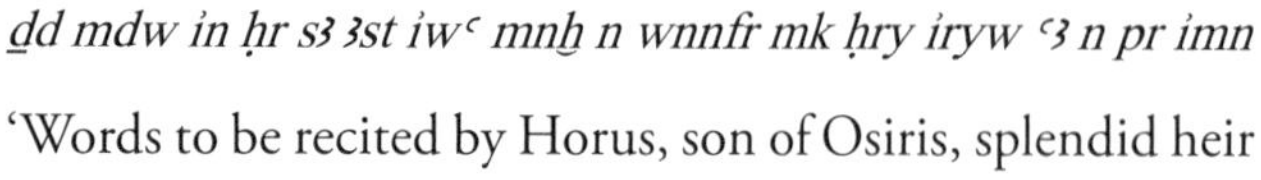

ḏd mdw in ḥr sꜣ ꜣst iwꜥ mnḫ n wnnfr mk ḥry iryw ꜥꜣ n pr imn imnmib[47]

'Words to be recited by Horus, son of Osiris, splendid heir of Wennufer: Look, (this is) the head door-keeper of the estate of Amun, Amenemib, justified.'

The gods are identified as 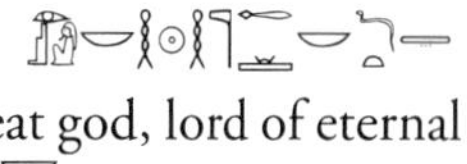 *wsir nb nḥḥ nṯr ꜥꜣ nb ḏt* 'Osiris, lord of eternity, great god, lord of eternal time'; 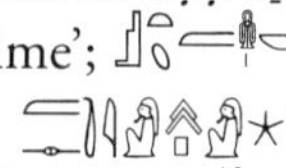 *ꜣst m sꜣ.k* 'Isis as your protection';  *nbtḥt* 'Nephthys';  *imst ḥp dwꜣmwtf kbḥ...* 'Amset, Hapy, Duamutef (and) Kebehsenuf'.[48]

43 In his copy Champollion inserted the third column of text as the second.

44 Wilkinson copied three little dots below the scales.

45 Wilkinson copied ▯ for ⊂ .

46 Rosellini (and Wilkinson) copied *t* for *m*.

47 Wilkinson copied a vertical line after the seated figure, possibly for *mꜣꜥ ḫrw*.

48 The jar is in Wilkinson's copy followed by three long vertical strokes. In Hay's copy of the scene (fig. (8), the upper part of the booth was drawn in pencil line too faint to copy.

Fig. 10 Wilkinson MSS v.212 [upper]

Right[49] wall
Upper register

Scene C

Gates and gate keepers[50]

Wilkinson MSS v.212; Champollion, *Not. descr.* i, pp. 533.

Wilkinson sketched three episodes from this register which featured the Book of Gates, the couple facing left towards three gate-keepers. Champollion also mentions three gate-keepers. In other instances, this number varies.

a) Deceased and wife arrive at a gate, facing left
Wilkinson MSS v.212 [upper and upper middle left] 'No. 1'.
She carries a stem of papyrus, while his hands are raised in adoration before a guardian with spear and knife, facing right, with an accompanying inscription imploring the gate-keeper to let them through:

iry ꜥꜣ[51] (sbḫt) tpy nty rn.f hꜣymꜥy

'Door-keeper of the first gate whose name is Haymay.' Wilkinson copied the hieroglyphs once more below his sketch.

Written in the opposite direction (left to right) are the following hieroglyphs:

→

iꜣw n kꜣ.k iry ꜥꜣ[52] sbḫt[53] n dwꜣt di.k ꜥk m ḥtp r st mꜣꜥt n kꜣ n wsir ḥri iryw ...(imn)mib mꜣꜥ ḫrw

'Praise to your ka, door-keeper (of the gate) of the Underworld. May you cause going in peace to the place of truth to the ka of Osiris, head [door-]keeper [Amen][54]emib, justified.'

Could one, perhaps, detect a slight pun here on the occupation of the tomb-owner – one colleague addressing another?

49 Sic Rosellini. Champollion has left wall ('paroi de gauche') for this scene (repeated by *Top. Bibl.*) but see further below.

50 See P. Barthelmess, *Die Übergang ins Jenseits in den thebanischen Beamtengräbern der Ramessidenzeit,* 1992, pp. 175ff.

51 The hieroglyph appears as a scroll.

52 The hieroglyph appears as *n*.

53 The signs are obscured by opaque tape.

54 As previous note.

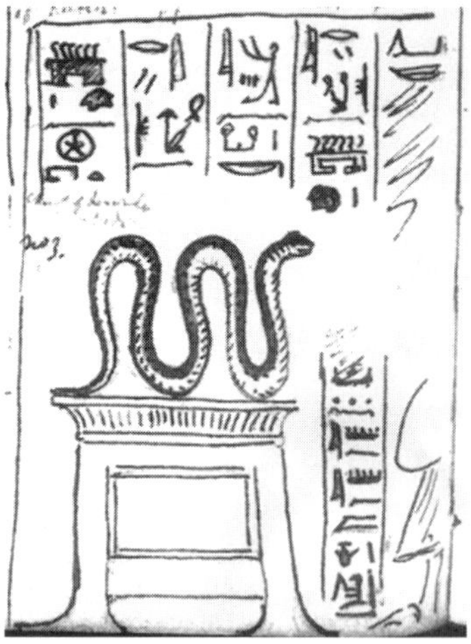

Fig. 11 Wilkinson MSS v.212 [middle]

Fig. 12 Wilkinson MSS v.212 [lower]

b) Ram-headed guardian at door with text
Wilkinson MSS v.212 [middle] 'No. 2'

The 'man and lady' stand, facing left, before another guardian of a gate. He has a ram's head and carries a large knife and spear like the previous door-keeper. He is

←

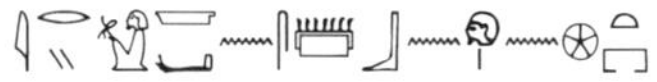

iry ꜥꜣ n sbḫt tpy n dwꜣt

'door-keeper of the first gate of the Underworld'

The inscription pertaining to the couple is as follows:

→

iꜣw n kꜣ.k iry tpy di.k ꜥḳ wstn.k[55] *mi wꜥ m tn r šms pꜣ nb imntt n kꜣ n ḥri iryw ꜥꜣ imnmib snt.f nbt pr ir[t]y(ꜥ)t*

'Praise to your ka, chief guardian. May you cause entering and travelling freely like one of you to follow the lord of the west to the ka of the chief door-keeper Amenemib (and) his wife, mistress of the house, Irtiꜥ(a)t.'

c) Serpent on shrine with text
Wilkinson MSS v.212 [lower] 'No. 3'

The serpent curls up on a stand with cavetto cornice. The tomb-owner stands before it. The serpent is

←

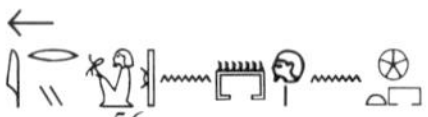

iry ꜥꜣ[56] *n sbḫt tpy n dwꜥt*

'Door-keeper of the first gate of the Underworld'

55 *Sic.* This appears to be an error on the part of the scribe – maybe for *nb*?
56 Copied as a scroll.

and the text before the tomb-owner

i͗3w n k3.k i͗ry n sbḫt tpy di.k…
'Adoration to your ka, keeper of the first gate. May you give…'

In front of the billowing garment of the tomb-owner is the following inscription:

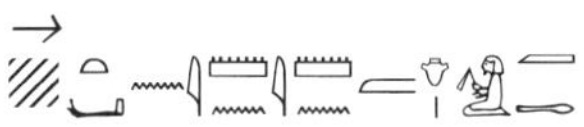

… ꜥ3 n i͗mn i͗mnmi͗b m3ꜥ ḫrw

'door-[keeper] of Amun, Amenemib, justified.'

According to Barthelmess,[57] the *sbḫt* gates should be open and the gate-keeper squatting inside. In this tomb, the gates, which are clearly *sbḫt* gates, are closed and the gate-keeper stands behind them (except in the case of the serpent). The human-headed standing gate-keeper seems to be less frequent than one with an animal's head.[58] The texts in our tomb are reduced to the bare minimum: a brief identification of the gate and a short prayer. All gates are labelled 'the first one'.
From a thematic point of view, the episodes at the gates precede the judgement before Osiris.[59] The two are sometimes juxtaposed, but in this tomb they occur on opposite walls (see further below).

Fig. 13 Wilkinson MSS v.211 [lower]

Right wall
Lower register, right[60]

Scene D
Offerings to deceased couple

Wilkinson MSS v.211 [lower] (inscriptions).
Champollion, *Not. descr.* i, p. 533, 851 (part of text).

The wall showed two offering scenes. Only one is mentioned by Champollion, but Wilkinson copied the texts of two. In both instances, judging from the directions of the hieroglyphs, the couple sat on chairs (cushions are mentioned by Champollion) facing right with a priest with 'leopard' skin opposite libating and censing to them on a large heap of offerings at their feet.

57 *Die Übergang ins Jenseits in den thebanischen Beamtengräbern der Ramessidenzeit*, p. 176.
58 Barthelmess, *op. cit.*, p. 180 n. 905 quotes only TT 157 and TT 409 for parallels.
59 P. Barthelmess, *Die Übergang ins Jenseits in den thebanischen Beamtengräbern der Ramessidenzeit*, 1992, pp. 175-81, esp. p. 180.
60 Champollion appears to imply that the scene is on the left wall, but see further below.

←
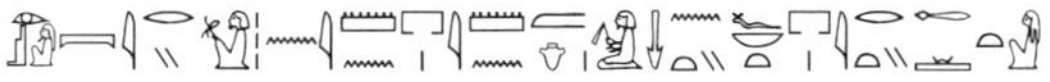

wsir ḥry iryw <ꜥꜣ> n imn imnmib snt.f nbt pr irtyꜥꜣt

'Osiris, head of (door)-keepers in the estate of Amun (and) his wife, mistress of the house, Irtiʿat.'
Above the priest:

→

irt ḥtp di nsw wdn ḫt nb nfrt wꜥbt šsp n.k mw m di n.k hꜥpy snw m di n.k ptḥ mꜣ rꜥ tnw ḫꜥꜥ.f sḏm.f sprt.k nb mꜣꜥ ḫrw

'Making an offering which the king gives, offering all good and pure things. Receive the water Hapy has given and loaves Ptah has given and see Ra each time he appears[61] that he may listen to your prayers concerning justification.'

The subject was repeated on the right, with the following inscription above the couple and priest, this time burning incense:

←

wsir ḥry iryw ꜥꜣ n pr imn imnmib snt.f nbt pr šmꜥyt n imn n mwt irtyꜥꜣt

'Osiris, head of door-keepers in the estate of Amun, Amenemib (and) his wife, mistress of the house, songstress of Amun and of Mut, Irtiʿat.'

→
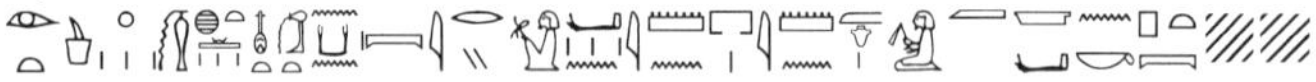

irt snṯr ḳbḥ ḫt nb nfrt wꜥbt n kꜣ n ḥry iryw <ꜥꜣ> n pr imn imnmib mꜣꜥ <ḫrw> wn n.k[62] *pt...*

'Performing (the act of offering) incense and cool water and all good and pure things to the ka of the head of [door-]keeper of the estate of Amun, Amenemib, justified. May heaven open for you...'

Left wall
Lower register(?)

Scene E

According to Champollion, *Not. descr.*, i, p. 533, this was 'seulement traité au trait rouge, et on avait déja mis les blancs.' But he gave no clue as to which subject was depicted. (As there seems to be some inconsistency in the use of right and left in his entry, it is just possible that this scene was on the opposite wall, see below.)

61 Wilkinson copied a short vertical stroke before the second [sign], at the beginning of a new column.
62 Copied as nb.

Uncertain position

Scene F

According to Rosellini, there must have been an additional gate-keeper somewhere: 'On the right, the deceased man and wife introduce themselves to "the keepers of the gates"' and he copied the following inscription.

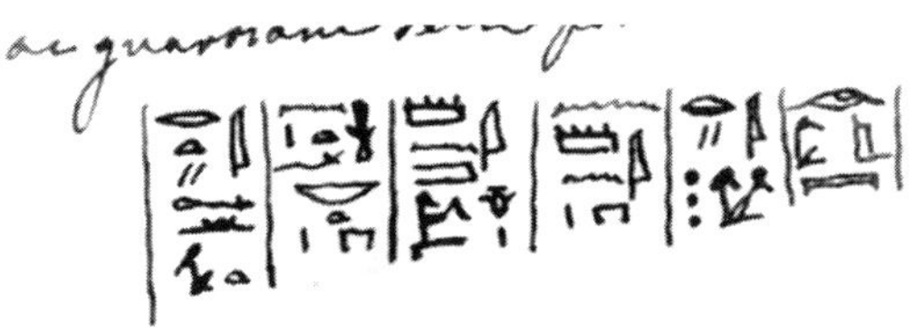

Fig. 14 Rosellini MSS 284, G53

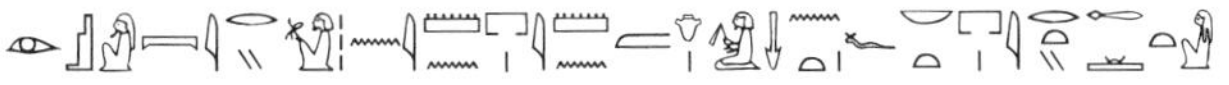

wsir ḥri̓ iryw n pr i̓mn i̓mnmi̓b snt.f nbt pr i̓rtyʿ3t

'Osiris, chief of (door-)keepers in the temple of Amun, Amenemib (and) his wife, mistress of the house, Irtiʿat.'

There is a slight problem here in that the inscription runs from right to left, i.e. the couple would be walking right and thus in the opposite direction from the previous three representations. Wilkinson and Champollion agree on three doorkeepers on the side wall. The disposition of the hieroglyphs on Rosellini's page does not correspond to any others copied in the tomb and must hence belong in an otherwise unrecorded scene, even when reversed.

Scene G

Below the above inscription, and with the caption 'elsewhere', Rosellini copied the following without further comment:

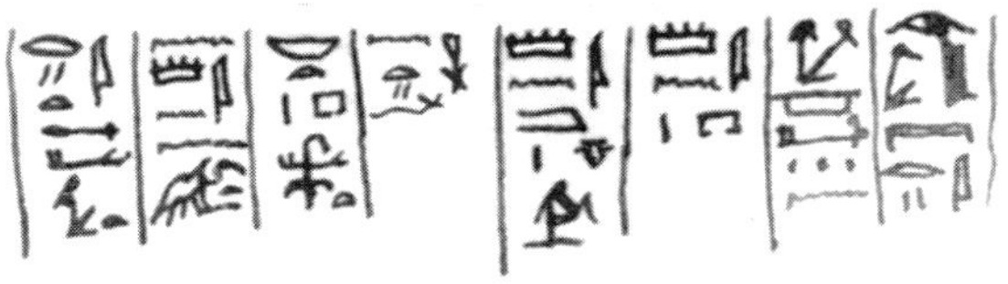

Fig. 15 Rosellini MSS 284, G53

←

wsir ḥri̓ iryw ʿ3 n pr i̓mn i̓mnmi̓b snt.f nbt pr šmʿyt n i̓mn n mwt i̓rtyʿ3t

'Osiris head of door-keepers in the temple of Amun, Amenemib (and) his wife, mistress of the house, songstress of Amun and of Mut, Irtiʿat.'

The couple would be facing right, but there is no way of telling whether they were active or passive.

Scale and position of the scenes

The dimensions of the tomb may be assessed from the facsimile drawing by Hay of the 'right' wall, in actual fact the left wall (see above and below). The decoration here took up 175 cm in width and 64.4 cm in height. The 'left' wall (i.e. the actual right wall), featuring in the upper register the couple before guardians of the Netherworld and below two representations of the deceased couple, would have taken up a similar amount of space. The height of the decorated surface would thus be ca. 65 cm x 2 = 130 cm plus an undecorated area below and possibly a dividing band between the two registers. These measurements would qualify for a chapel called a 'chambrette' by Champollion and a 'piccola stanzetta' by Rosellini.

The decoration on the left wall would be distributed as in Ramessid 'naos' stelae with the couple being active in the upper register, adoring deities, and passive in the lower register which is concerned with the funerary cult.[63] If the information given in the *Top. Bibl.*, quoting Champollion, were taken at face value, the orientation of the scenes would be the opposite of what one would have expected for a Theban tomb with its entrance more or less to the east. Fortunately the notebook of Rosellini clarifies this problem. The weighing and conducting scene (A and B) should belong on the left wall, upper register, and the three guardians of the gates of the Underworld (C) on the right wall, upper register.[64] The two scenes showing a priest offering to the deceased couple (D) would belong in the lower right register. This leaves the unfinished offering scene (E) for the lower left, although Champollion indicates this as being on the right. Two scenes are unaccounted for: F with the couple facing right before a gate-keeper and G, another scene with the couple facing right. None of the early travellers mentioned anything about the rear and front walls, except that Champollion said that 'the rest of the tomb was without paintings'.

63 J. Assmann, 'Helligt rum i ramessidiske privatgrave', 2000, p. 5, an article based on a lecture given at the British Museum Colloquium in London in 2000, now published in N. Strudwick and J. H. Taylor (eds.), *The Theban Necropolis. Past, Present and Future,* 2003, pp. 46-52, esp. p. 49.

64 Gates are most frequently near the entrance of the tomb (P. Barthelmess, *Die Übergang ins Jenseits in den thebanischen Beamtengräbern der Ramessidenzeit*, 1992, p. 184).

TT A16

Among the early travellers, only Hay and his team paid a visit to this tomb to copy the scenes on the walls. This is surprising in view of the fact that a substantial amount of wall-decoration appears to have survived in excellent condition until his day. The tomb was located 'near Piccinini's house' in Draᶜ abu el-Nagaᶜ.

The main feature of the wall-decoration as recorded in the Hay MSS is a lengthy extract from the Book of the Dead. In all, 280 vertical columns of text were copied along with accompanying vignettes above. The sheets of tracings done by Hay and his assistants have been matched by the present writer to form one short and two large continuous sections of text. Three sheets show additional vignettes. Furthermore Hay's team copied a large scene with a rounded top showing the tomb-owner before two aspects of Osiris and another with just one figure of the tomb-owner which is very similar to the one on the right in the previous scene and with identical accompanying text.
A figure of a drummer (Hay MSS 29851, 128), said by the *Top. Bibl.* to have come from this tomb, was found to be so similar to a painting in TT 65 (a tomb also known to early travellers)[65] that in the opinion of the present writer this is undoubtedly the original position of the figure.
A number of the drawings have in recent years been published by the present writer (see under the individual scenes below).

The owner of the tomb

Dhutihotpe  the tomb-owner, is the only person mentioned in the tomb as recorded in the Hay MSS. Apart from being frequently referred to as  *sš nsw mꜣᶜ mr.f* true scribe of the king whom he loves', Dhutihotpe was  *imy-r pr wr n niwt rst* 'great steward of the Southern City', a title occasionally abbreviated to *imy-r pr wr*, or just *imy-r pr*. But he was also  *imy-r pr wr n Imn* 'great steward of Amun', as well as  *imy-r pr ḥḏ n Imn* 'overseer of the treasury of Amun' and  'overseer of the treasury of the Lord of the Two Lands' (col. 260 of the Book of the Dead). To these were added the duties of  *imy-r šnwty n Imn-Rᶜ* 'overseer of the two granaries of Amun-Ra' and 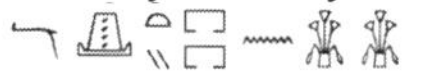 'overseer of the two granaries of the South and the North' (cols. 243 and 260 of the Book of the Dead), and, for specific occasions,  *sšm ḥb n Imn-Rᶜ* 'leader of festivals of Amun-Ra' (col. 260 of the Book of the Dead), or even  *sšm ḥb n nṯrw nbw Ipt-swt* 'leader of festivals of all the gods in Karnak' (col. 267 of the Book of the Dead) (var. 'of all the gods in Thebes": col. 244 of the Book of the Dead).
Thus our tomb-owner was a man of some standing in the administration of the palace, in the temple of Amun at Thebes, and in the service of his king. The inscriptions give no further clue to a more exact date for Dhutihotpe's activities, but it would seem that he functioned somewhere between the reigns of Ramesses II and III.[66]

65 See photograph in L. Manniche, *Ancient Egyptian Musical Instruments,* 1975, fig. 6. The tomb is being studied by a Hungarian mission (see e.g. *Seventh International Congress of Egyptologists*, Cambridge, 3-9 September 1995, pp. 8-9 (contribution by T. A. Bács) and *Tenth International Congress of Egyptologists*, Rhodes 22–29 May 2008, pp. 264-5 (contribution by K. Vértes)).

66 F. Kampp, *Die thebanische Nekropole*, p. 617 suggests '19th dyn.?'

Fig. 16 Hay MSS 29851, 129, 131-7
(re-drawn by LM)

The decoration of the tomb

Scene A
The tomb-owner before two aspects of Osiris

Hay MSS 29851, 129, 131-7; Manniche, *City of the Dead*, fig. 67;[67] Manniche in *Papyrus* 17/2, 1997, p. 16, fig. 8.

The nature of the decoration suggests that it occupied more or less the entire width of a wall, possibly with a subscene not recorded (for the dimensions, see below). The representation is symmetrical with variations in the details, showing two aspects of Osiris seated back to back in a kiosk surmounted by a winged disc. To each of the deities the tomb-owner presents a bouquet.
Some of the colours were noted on the facsimile drawing in French.[68] In both instances the complexion of Osiris was green, the background colour on the right being red. The remaining colours are as would be expected.
To the left, the text above Osiris runs as follows:

67 This drawing, with damaged parts restored, has also been used as decoration on a T-shirt printed by the Egyptological Society in Brazil.
68 Suggesting that this copy was probably done by Dupuy.

→

ḏd mdw ỉn wsỉr ḫnty ỉmntt wnnfr ḥk{t} ꜥnḫw]{t} nsw r nḥḥ

‘Words spoken by Osiris, foremost in the West, Wennufer, ruler of the living, king for eternal time *(nḥḥ)*.

The god is dressed in a garment with a dotted pattern, and he wears a black wig with uraeus and white crown.
To the right the god wears a feathered garment and white crown, and in addition to sceptre and flagellum, he holds a ribbed palm leaf. The inscription says:

←

ḏd mdw ỉn wsỉr ḫnty ỉmntt nṯr ꜥꜣ ḥkꜣ ḏt

‘Words spoken by Osiris, foremost in the West, great god, ruler of eternity’.

The phrases actually spoken by the deities (implied by *ḏd mdw*) were omitted. The two representations of Dhutihotpe show him in different garments and wigs. The figure on the left, perhaps painted by a different artist, indicates eyelids and wrinkles on the throat. In fact, the two faces are by no means identical, and we must take it that two painters were at work on this wall, each with his individual touch.
The elaborate bouquets consist of stems of papyrus with tiered collars made of floral or other material. The one on the left has an additional floral collar and includes at the top two of the flowers often interpreted as poppy.

Inscription on the left:

←

rdỉ ỉꜣw n wsỉr wnnfr ḫnty Igrt nb nḥḥ ḥkꜣ ḏt dỉ.k prt ḫrw t ḥkt kꜣw ꜣpdw kbḥ ỉrp ỉrtt mnḫt snṯr mrḥt ḫt nb nfr(t) wꜥb(t) n kꜣ n wsỉr sšm ḥb n ỉmn-rꜥ ỉmy-r pr wr ḏhwtyḥtp

‘Giving praise to Osiris Wennufer, foremost in Igeret, lord of eternal time *(nḥḥ)*, ruler of eternity *(ḏt)*. May you give an invocation offering of bread, beer, oxen, fowl, cold water, wine, milk, cloth, incense, *mrḥt*--unguent, all good and clean things to the ka of Osiris, leader of festivals of Amun-Ra, great steward, Dhutihotpe.’

Inscription on the right:

→

ỉỉn(ỉ) m ỉꜣw n wsỉr ỉnk wḏꜣ tp tꜣ ỉw ỉry.ỉ n.k mꜣꜥt rꜥ nb ỉw.ỉ rḫ.kwỉ ꜥnḫ.k ỉm.s dỉ.k mw t ṯꜣw n wsỉr ỉmy-r pr ḏhwtyḥtp mꜣꜥ ḫrw

‘(I) have come in praise to Osiris. I was one prosperous on earth having done right for you every day, because I know that you live on it (sc. maat). May you

give water, bread and breath to Osiris, steward Dhutihotpe, justified.'
On Hay's facsimile copy, the height of this scene, from the lower line of the mat to the apex of the lunette, is 81.3 cm, the width being around 100 cm.

Scene B
The tomb-owner with bouquet before [Osiris]

Hay MSS 29851,130, 138-9; L. Manniche, *An Ancient Egyptian Herbal,* 1987/2006, fig. p. 25; id. in *Papyrus* 17/2, 1997, figs. 9 (original Hay tracing of upper part) and 10.
On Hay's facsimile copy the scene measures 91.4 x ca. 28 cm (with tip of sandal restored).
In this picture the garment and wig correspond to the reverse representation (facing right) of Dhutihotpe in scene A, whereas the text is absolutely identical to that of the tomb-owner facing left, although there is some variation in the way in which the hieroglyphs have been distributed over the available space. The bouquet combines elements from both of those in scene A. In addition to the three stems of papyrus, two red 'poppies' are inserted at the top along with a 'looped' flower, repeated below. The deity to whom the flowers are presented was not copied, but according to the text it was once more Osiris, each hieroglyph being identical to those of the previous scene:

i͗n(i͗) m i͗ꜥw n Wsi͗r i͗nk wḏꜣ tp tꜣ i͗w i͗ry.i͗ n.k mꜣꜥt rꜥ nb i͗w.i͗ rḫ.kwi͗ ꜥnḫ.k i͗m.s di͗.k mw t ṯꜣw n Wsi͗r i͗my-r pr ḏhwtyḥtp mꜣꜥ ḫrw

'(I) have come in praise to Osiris. I was one prosperous on earth having done right for you every day. I know what you live on. May you give water, bread and breath to Osiris, steward Dhutihotpe, justified.'

Fig. 17 Hay MSS 29851, 130, 138-9 (re-drawn by LM)

Scene C
Book of the Dead [figs. 18-25]

Section A
159 cols. of text on the following sheets of the Hay MSS assembled from left to right, the text to be read in this direction: MSS 29851, 118, 122, 123, 124, 127, 126, 125, 107, 108, 104, 111, 116, 112, 105, 109. It is apparent that in the British Library the sheets were numbered with no regard to their logical sequence.

Section B
81 cols. of text, to be read from right to left, on the following sheets assembled from right to left: MSS 29851, 105, 117, 103, 113, 106, 114, 116.

Section C
40 cols. of text written from left to right on the following sheets assembled from left to right: MSS 29851, 115, 121, 120, 119.

The hieroglyphs in the vertical text columns all face right. But whereas in sections A and C they are to be read from left to right, *i.e.* retrograde, in B they read in the opposite direction from right to left.[69] The text columns of A have been numbered from **(1)** to **(159)**; in B and C the numbering continues directly as [160]ff., but in brackets to indicate that part of the text is known to be missing.

The right part of A contains approximately the first half of the long Spell 17, whereas the last third or so of the same chapter appears to the right on B, making altogether 221 columns of Spell 17. Both right extremities of the two sections suggest that this was the end of the wall, for the vignettes conclude neatly in the same place as the text. The last column on A contains the end of a phrase, whereas the first column on B begins with '*Otherwise said:*'. The missing part of the full Spell 17 would have taken up only part of one wall, however narrow. On the basis of the available evidence it would thus appear that the ancient scribe adapted the copy of the actual scroll before him to the wall-space at his disposal and simply omitted part of the text.

Both sections A and B continued on the left beyond Hay's copies. On section C, the same pattern is discernible: on the left we have the concluding line of a previous chapter, whereas on the right a chapter comes to the end. In addition, the dividing vertical line is here clearly marked by the copyist, whereas elsewhere he only indicated the top and bottom end.

This state of affairs suggests that we are dealing with the right part of wall (or two adjoining walls) of which sections A, B and C formed three registers. From a contextual point of view A and B belong together. In theory A could be above B, or vice versa. A faint clue to B being above, and the text to be read from below, is the fact that the wall appears to taper slightly inwards on B.

Section A

Bibliography: Cols. 65-76 and the vignette with the cow and sacred eye appeared in *Papyrus* 1997/2, p. 14, fig. 4. The cat slaying a serpent in Hay MSS 29851,112 was published in L. Manniche, *City of the Dead,* fig. 51.

Cols. 1-14 contain Spell 23 of the Book of the Dead concerning the Opening of the Mouth. The two vignettes above on the wall are not immediately relevant to the text, for they show on the left the tomb-owner adoring  *wsỉr nb nḥḥ ḥkꜣ ḏ(t)*' 'Osiris, lord of eternity, ruler of everlasting time' and, on the right, adoration of the Phoenix:  *ỉnk bnw bꜣ n rꜥ* 'I am *bnw*, soul of R' (cf. col. A8 of the text). It would seem that a sheet is missing from the Hay MSS, for only part of the tomb-owner appears on our first sheet. He is identified as  *sšm ḥb ỉm[n]-rꜥ* 'leader of festivals of Amun-Ra'. On the right he is named as  *wsỉr [ỉmy-]r n nỉwt rst ḏhwtyḥtp* 'Osiris, steward of the Southern City, Dhutihotpe'. All the vignettes are in full colour, the bird being the conventional blue.

Following the concluding signs of a preceding spell  the text runs as follows (rubrics being here marked in italics) with the signs positioned in the opposite direction as to that of the reading:[70]

(1) '*Spell of Opening the Mouth* of Osiris Dhutihotpe, justified, to give his magic spells in the Underworld. My mouth is opened by Ptah and what was on my mouth has been loosened by my local god. Thoth comes indeed, filled and equipped with magic, after having loosened the bonds that Seth made which were on my mouth, when he contended against Atum and [placed]

69 Cf. H. G. Fischer, *L'écriture et l'art de l'Egypte ancienne*, 1986, pp. 105-30; R. B. Parkinson, *Cracking Codes*, 1999, p. 57.

70 The translation largely follows that of R. O. Faulkner, *The Ancient Egyptian Book of the Dead*, 1985.

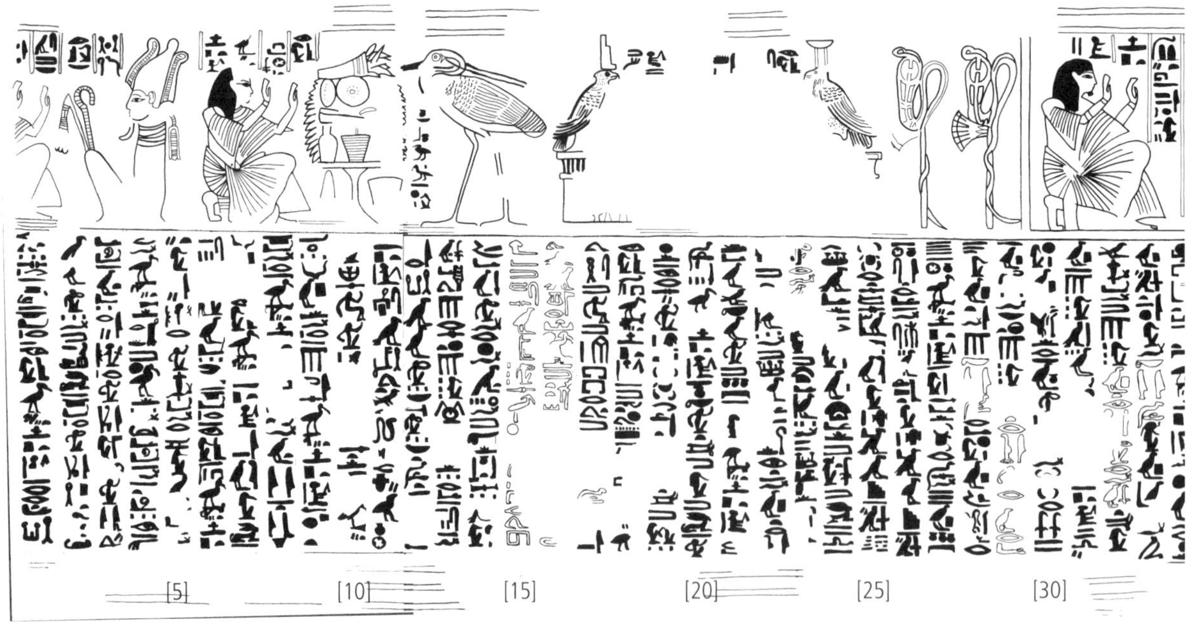

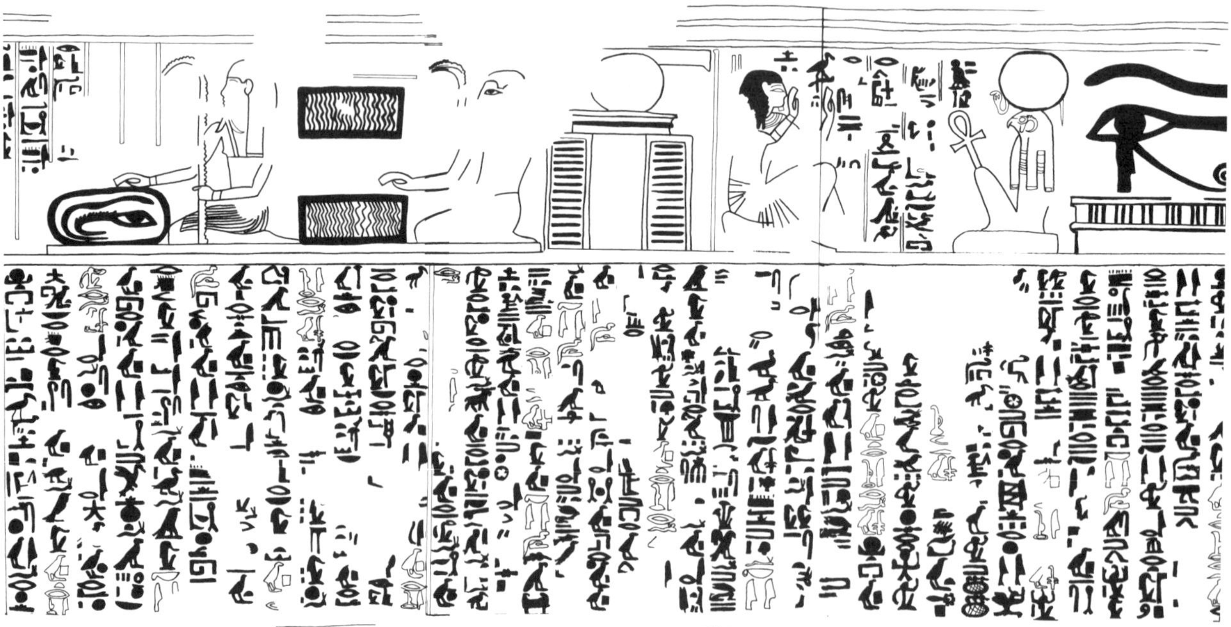

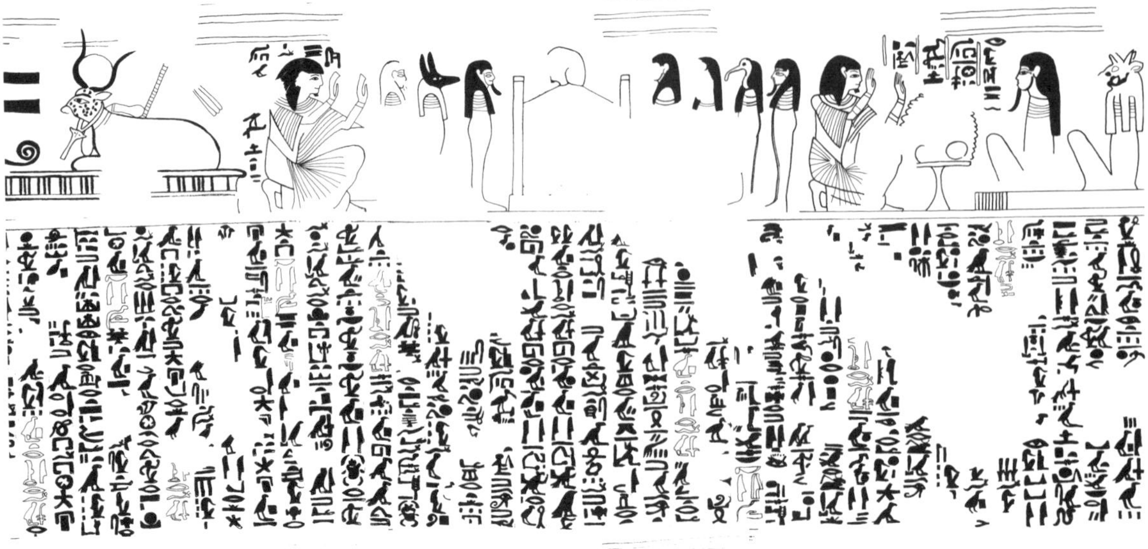

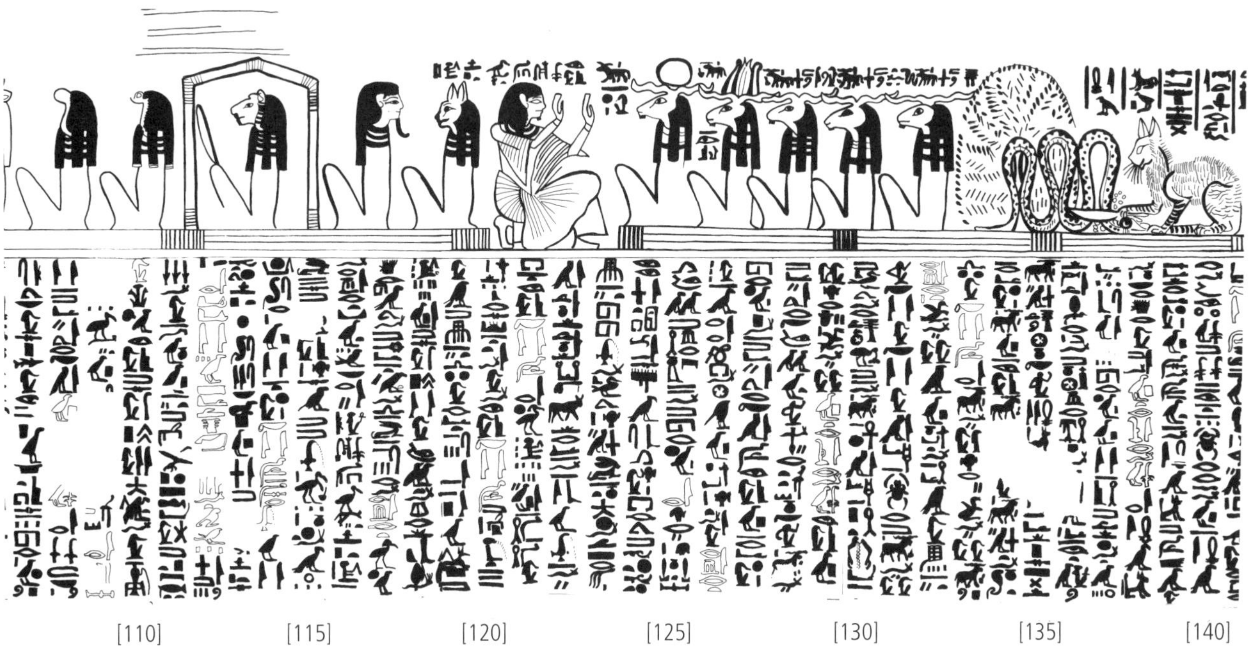

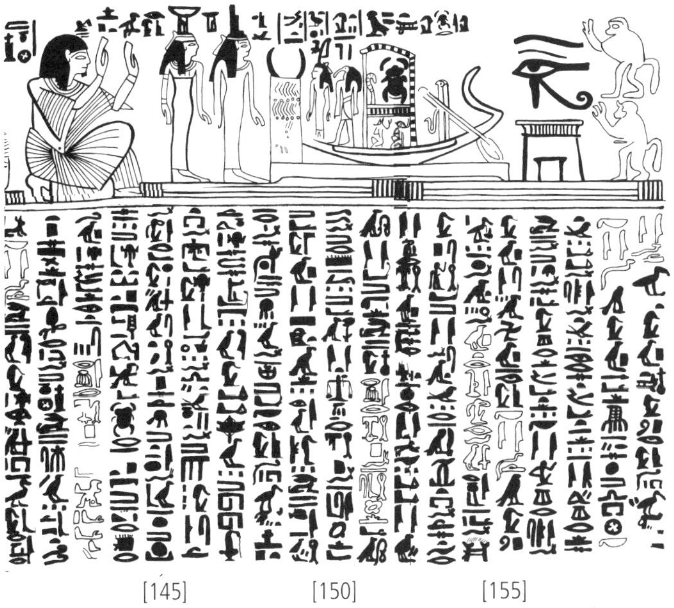

Figs. 18-22.
Section A cols. 1-159

them [as guardians]. **(5)** The mouth of Osiris steward Dhutihotpe is opened, [the mouth] of Osiris Dhutihotpe is split open by Shu. He opened the mouth of Dhutihotpe with that instrument of bronze with which he split open the mouths of the gods. Dhutihotpe is Sakhmet, **(10)** and I sit beside Her [who is in the] great [wind] of the sky. Dhutihotpe is Orion the Great who is amongst the souls of Heliopolis. As for any magic spell or any words which may be said against [Dhuti-]hotpe, the gods will rise up against it and the entire Ennead. They have given him his justification against his enemies before the tribunal like Ra.'

Cols. 15-159 contain the first half of the lengthy Spell 17 which, as explained above, continued in another register.[71] The vignettes illustrating the spell are the following:

Isis and Nephthys as kites protecting the mummy of the tomb-owner. The latter is destroyed, but the inscription above remained:

71 See U. Rößler-Köhler, *Kapitel 17 des ägyptischen Totenbuches*, 1979.

wsir s...b n ỉmn-rꜥ [...] mꜣꜥ ẖrw m ỉmꜣẖ(?)
'Osiris, l[eader of festi[vals] of Amun-Ra [Dhutihotpe], justified as a revered one(?).'
The two kites were red. On their right are the two cobras on poles.
Then follows a vignette showing Dhutihotpe adoring the sacred eye and two water gods. The inscriptions pertaining to the latter were not copied and the columns for the text remain empty. Elsewhere (cols. 65-6) the lakes are identified as the Lake of Natron and the Lake of Maat. The hieroglyphs in front of the tomb-owner are
wsir ỉmy-r pr [wr ỉmy-r pr] ḥḏ n ỉmn-rꜥ sšm ḥb n ỉmn-rꜥ ỉmy-r šnwty n ỉmn-rꜥ ḏhwtyḥtp mꜣꜥ ẖrw 'Osiris, reat steward, [treasurer] of Amun-Ra, leader of festivals of Amun-Ra, overseer of the two granaries of Amun-Ra Dhutihotpe, justified.'
Separating this vignette from the following there is an open gateway with the sun appearing above. To the right the tomb-owner now adores a figure of Ra-Harakhti 'Ra-Harakhti (followed by *nṯr* (determinative?))', and the celestial cow with a large sacred eye placed before it (cf. cols. 95 ff.). The accompanying text reads:

ỉꜣw n rꜥ wb[n].f di.k ꜥk pr ỉmi ẖri-nṯr nn šnꜥ.tw bꜣ wsir sš [nsw] mꜣꜥ mr.f ỉmy-r pr ḏhwtyḥtp mꜣꜥ ẖrw 'Adoration to Ra in his rising. May you give going in and going out (to the one) in the Underworld. May his soul not be turned back (to) Osiris, true scribe of the king whom he loves, steward Dhutihotpe, justified.'
Our tomb-owner is next seen adoring a chest with a human head flanked by three plus four mummiform figures. In other copies of the Book of the Dead there are only four figures, identified as the four sons of Horus. Dhutihotpe is ... *sš nsw mꜣꜥ mr.f ỉmy-r pr wr n [...] ḏhwtyḥtp mꜣꜥ ẖrw* 'true scribe of the king whom he loves, great steward of [...], Dhutihotpe.'
The tomb-owner proceeds to worship a group of deities, the first four having the heads of a man, a cow, and two with serpents' heads. A lion-headed god is seated in a booth, while a human-headed deity turns his head towards a figure with the head of a cat. None of these figures have identifying inscriptions, but the tomb-owner has his usual *wsir sš nsw mꜣꜥ mr.f ỉmy-r pr n niwt rst ḏhwtyḥtp , mꜣꜥ [ẖrw]* 'Osiris, true scribe of the king whom he loves, steward of the Southern City, Dhutihotpe, justified'.
Adoration is then given to five ram-headed figures and the familiar cat slaying a serpent under the *ỉšd*-tree. *wsir sš nsw ỉmy-r pr ḏhwtyḥtp* 'Osiris, royal scribe, steward Dhutihotpe' faces the deities named as 'Soul of Ra', 'Soul of Osiris', 'Soul which is in Shu', 'Soul which is in Tefenet' and 'Soul which is in Mendes'. The cat is *miw pw ꜥꜣ psš.s ỉšd r gs.f m ỉwnw* 'The great cat which split the *ỉšd*-tree on its side in Heliopolis' (cf. cols. 135ff.). The serpent is blue with black markings, the cat yellow with red lines.

The final vignette of this section of the Book of the Dead shows *wsir ḏḥwtyḥtp mꜣꜥ ẖrw* 'Osiris Dhutihotpe, justified' adoring the solar boat which has in it a sceptre and a scarab 'Ra-Harakhti-Atum-

Khepri' and the gods  *mꜣꜥt sꜣt rꜥ* 'Maat, daughter of Ra' and  *ḏḥwty nb mdw nṯr* 'Thoth, lord of divine speech'. Isis and Nephthys stand guard, while on the extreme right two baboons raise their arms to a sacred eye on a shrine (cf. col. 248 where the solar baboons of Isis and Nephthys are referred to.)

This is clearly the end of the register, for the horizontal line dividing the vignettes from the text below terminates at this point. Although the text of Spell 17 is only half completed, the end of the register coincides neatly with the end of a phrase.

Spell 17

(15) 'The beginning of the praises and glorifications, going in and going *out of the Underworld, being a spirit in the* [*beautiful*] *West* [...(verb of motion)], sitting in the booth, going out of [...] *To be recited* by Osiris steward Dhutihotpe, justified, after he has died [...]. It is beneficial to him who does it on earth.
Now came into being [all] the words of the [lord of] all beings. **(20)** Words to be recited (by) Dhutyhotpe, justified: I am Atum when I was alone in Nun, Dhutyhotpe, justified. (I was) Ra in his appearings when he began to rule what he has made. What *does it mean?* It means Ra in his appearings when he began *to rule what he* [*had made*], when Ra began to appear as king, before **(25)** the supports of Shu had come into being on the terrace hill which is in Hermopolis, when he had placed the children of weakness on the terrace hill which is in Hermopolis.
Dhutihotpe (is) the great god who created himself. (He) is water, (he) is Nun, father of the gods. *Otherwise said*: He is Ra who created his names, Lord of the Ennead. *Who is he? It is Ra* **(30)** who created his names and his [members]; it is the coming into existence of those gods who are in [his suite]. [Dhuti]hotpe (is) the one who is not opposed among the gods.
Who is he? He is Atum who is in his sun-disc. *Otherwise said*: He is Ra when he rises in the eastern horizon of the sky. Dhutihotpe (is) yesterday. He knows (35) tomorrow. (Here follows an erroneous duplicate writing: 'Lord of All (and) his son Horus was made to rule.').
What does it mean? As for yesterday, that is Osiris. As for tomorrow, that is Ra on that day on which the enemies of the Lord of All were destroyed and his son Horus was made to rule. *Otherwise said*: That is the day of the 'We remain' festival, **(40)** when the burial of Osiris was ordered by his father Ra.
The battle-gound of the gods was made in accordance with the command of Osiris, Lord of the [des]ert.
What does it mean? It is the West. It was made for the [souls] of the gods in accordance with the command of Osiris, Lord of the Western desert. [*Otherwise said*: It means that this is] the West to which Ra made every god descend, and he fought [the Two for it].
Osiris **(45)** Dhutihotpe knows that [great] god who is in it.
Who is he? [He is Osiris...] His name is Ra. His name is Praise-of-Ra. He is the soul of Ra with whom he himself copulated.
Dhutihotpe is that great phoenix which is in Heliopolis, the supervisor of what exists.

Who is he? He is Osiris(?) *Otherwise said*: It is his corpse. **(50)** *Otherwise said*: His wounds. As for that which exists, it is his corpse. *Otherwise said*: [It means eternity *(nḥḥ)* and] everlasting time *(ḏt)*. As for eternity, it means the day; as for everlasting time, it means the night.
[Dhutihotpe is] Min in his going forth. I have placed the plumes on my head.
What does it mean? As for [Min], he is Horus who protected his father. As for his going forth, it means his birth. As for [his] plumes on **(55)** [his head] Isis and Nephthys [went] and placed (themselves) behind him when they were the Two Kites, and they were firm on his head. *Otherwise said*: It is the great uraeus which is on the brow of their father Atum. *Otherwise said*: The two plumes on his head are his eyes.
When I was in [my] land I came into my town.
What is it? It is the horizon **(60)** of [my father Atum]. I destroy wrongdoing (against) me and dispel [what was done evilly against me].
What does it mean? It means that the umbilical chord of the royal scribe and steward Dhutihotpe will be cut. I was [cleansed] in the two [...] pools [which are in] Heracleopolis on the day of the oblation by the people to that Great God who is in them. What are they?[72] Million **(65)** is the name of one; Sea is the name of the other. They are the Lake of Natron and the Lake of Maat. *Otherwise said*: Million Governs is the name of one, Sea is the name of the other. As for that great god who is in them, he is Ra himself.
I go on the [road] which I know in front of the Island of the Just. *What is it?* It is Ro **(70)** setau. The southern [gate] is in Naref, the northern gate is in the two mounds of Osiris. As for the Island of the Just, it is Abydos. *Otherwise said*: It is the road on which my father Atum went when he proceeded to the Field of the Rushes.
I arrive at the Island of the Horizon-dwellers, I go out from the holy gate.
What is it? **(75)** It is the Field of Rushes which produced the provisions for the gods, who are round about [the shrine]. As for that holy [gate], it is the gate of the Supports of Shu. As for the holy gate, it is the gate of Duat. *Otherwise said*: It is the doors through which Atum went, when he proceeded to the eastern horizon of the sky.
O you who are in my presence. Give me your hands for I, for I am that one who came into being **(80)** amongst you.
What does it mean? It means the blood which fell from [the phallus of] Ra when he took to cutting himself. Then there came into being [the gods who are] in his presence, who are authority [and intelligence] and they [shall] follow after Atum daily. **(85)** [...] Osiris, steward Dhutihotpe [has taken hold] of the sacred eye after it had been injured on that day when rivals fought.
What does it mean? It means the day when Horus fought with Seth when he inflicted injury on Horus' face and when Horus took away Seth's testicles. It was **(90)** [Thoth who] did this with his fingers. (I) lifted up the hair from the sacred eye at its time of wrath.
What does it mean? It means the right [eye of Ra when it rages against him after he had sent] it out. It was Thoth who lifted up the hair [from it when he fetched it in good condition] without it having suffered any harm. *Otherwise said*: It means that his [eye] was sick when it wept a second time, and Thoth spat upon it.
I have seen this sun god **(95)** who was born yesterday from the buttocks of the

72 The text has 'What is it?'

celestial cow; if he be well, then [I] will be well [...].
What does it mean? It means these waters of the sky. [*Otherwise said*:] It is the image of the Eye of Ra on the morning of his [daily] birth. [As for] the celestial cow, she is the sacred eye **(100)** of Ra every day of [...]. [Because I am one of those] gods who are in the suite of Horus who spoke [...] his Lord [...].
Who are they?[73] *(They are) Imsety* [Hapy, Duamutef and Qebeh]senuef. Hail to you, Lords... tribunal which is behind Osiris, who put terror into the doers of wrong, who are in the suite of Her who makes content and protects.**(105)** Here I am: I have come to you that you may drive out all the evil which is on me just as you did for those seven spirits who are in the suite of the Lord of Sepa, whose places Anubis made ready on that day of 'Come here!'
Who are they?[74] As for those Lords [...] they are Thoth ... West. *As for the tribunal* **(110)** which is behind Osiris, Imsety, Hapy, Duamutef and Qebehsenuef, it is these who are behind the Great Bear in the northern sky. *As for those who put terror into the doers of wrong*, who are in the suite of Her who makes content and protects, they are Sobk and those who are in [the waters]. As for Her who makes content and protects, she is the eye of Ra. *Otherwise said*: *She is a flame* which **(115)** follows after Osiris, burning up the souls of his enemies.
As for all the evil which is on the royal scribe, steward Dhutihotpe, justified, ever since he came down from his mother's womb, never did it exist. As for these seven spirits, Imsety, Hapy, he who sees his father, He who is under the moringa tree, and Horus the Eyeless, it is they who were set by Anubis as a protection for the burial of Osiris. *Otherwise said*: Behind the embalming place **(120)** of his father Osiris. *Otherwise said*: As for these seven spirits, they are Nedjehnedjeh, Imkedked, Bull whose flame was set for him in front of his burning, he who entered into him who is in his hour, the Red-eyes who is in the Mansion of Red Linen, the Radiant one who comes out after having turned **(125)** back, He who sees in the night what he shall bring by day. *As for* the head of this tribunal (it is) Naref, it is Horus who protected his father. *As for* that day of 'Come to (me)' it means that Osiris said to Ra: 'Come to me that I may see you – so said he of the West.'
I am the twin souls which are within the Two Fledglings.
Who is he? He is Osiris **(130)** when he entered into Mendes. He found the living soul there and they embrace each other there. Then his twin soul came into being. *As for* the Two Fledglings they are Horus the protector of his father and Horus the Eyeless. *Otherwise said*: As for his twin souls within the Two Fledglings, they are the soul of Ra, the soul of Osiris, the soul [which is in Shu], the soul which is in Nut, **(135)** the soul which is in Mendes.
I am the [great] cat who split the *išd*-tree on its side in Heliopolis on that night of making war on behalf of those who warded off the rebels on that day in which were destroyed the enemies of the Lord of All. *What does it mean?* As for the great cat, he is Ra himself, who was called Cat when Sia spoke about him. He was cat-like[75] in what he did, and that was how his name of cat came into being. **(140)** *Otherwise said*: (It means) that Shu is making an inventory for Geb. As for the splitting of the *išd*-tree on its side in Heliopolis, it was when the children of weakness carried out what they did. *As for that night of making war*, it *means that they entered* **(145)** into the east of the sky, and war broke out in the entire sky and earth.
O Ra who are in your egg, shining in your disc, rising in your horizon, swimming over your firmament, having no equal among the gods, sailing over the

73 The text has 'what is it?'
74 The text has 'what is it?'
75 Written in this copy as a cognate of the root *mꜣꜣ*, 'see'.

supports of Shu, giving air with the breath of your mouth, illuminating the Two Lands with your sunshine, may you save Osiris steward Dhutihotpe from that god whose shape is secret, whose eyebrows **(150)** are the arms of the balance, on that night of reckoning up the robbers in front of Wennufer. *As for that night of reckoning up* the robbers it is the night of the flame against the fallen, when the lasso was put on the wrong-doers at his slaughter-house for killing the souls of his enemies.
Who is he? As to the one who brought his hand it is Shesmu, **(155)** he is the mutilator of Osiris. *Otherwise said*: He is Horus, he has two heads, one bearing right, the other bearing wrong. He gives wrong to whoever does it and right to whoever brings it. *Othertwise said*: he is Horus the Great, pre-eminent in Letopolis. *Otherwise said*: He is Thoth, he is Nefertum. Osiris steward Dhutihotpe.'

Section B

Cols. [160]-[236] contain the end of Spell 17, with Spell 20 following on directly in col. [236] until the bottom of col. [240].
The vignettes, read from right to left as the text below, begin with a scene showing the tomb-owner *wsir imy-r pr imy-r pr ḥḏ n imn rꜥ ḏḥwtyḥtp mꜣꜥ ḫrw* 'Osiris steward, overseer of the treasury of Amun-Ra Dhutihotpe, justified' adoring a demon *ꜥm ḥḥ rn.f* '"swallower of millions"[76] is his name' across a lake of flames (cf. cols. [164]ff.). Behind follows a recumbent lion on a shrine called *mꜣi ḥḏ r* 'Lion bright of mouth' (cf. cols. [211] and [229]). The body of the lion is yellow and it rests on a white plinth with a blue cushion or mat. Two deities with serpents' heads squat behind. They are labeled [77] 'Nehebkau' 'Osiris, Lord of eternity'. A goose and a falcon alighting complete the scene. The tip of the falcon's wings protrudes a little beyond the line, indicating the end of the scene. The part of the spell which the serpents and birds illustrate is omitted in Hay's copy: 'I fly up as a falcon, I cackle as a goose, I pass eternity like Nehebkau.' If the missing columns of text were actually included in the tomb, as suggested above, the vignette would have been in the vicinity of the portion of the spell which it illustrates.
The next scene is a wide one showing *wsir sš nsw mꜣꜥ mr.f ḏḥwtyḥtp mꜣꜥ ḫrw* 'Osiris true scribe of the king whom he loves, Dhutihotpe, justified' adoring eleven squatting deities, each of them clearly identified: 1) (falcon-headed) *skri*[78] *wsir nb nḥḥ*. 'Sokar-Osiris, Lord of eternity'; 2) human-headed 'Isis, Divine mother, Mistress of heaven, Lady of all lands'; 3) *imsti mry wsir* 'Imseti, beloved of Osiris'; 4) (lion-headed) *ḥpy mḥ ib wsir mry* (?) 'Hapy who pleases Osiris, beloved of(?) … (?)'; 5) (human-headed) *tmw nb tꜣwy iwny* 'Atum, Lord of the Two Lands, the Heliopolitan'; 6) (human-headed) 'Shu'; 7) (human-headed) 'Tefenet'; 8) (human-headed) *wsir ḥkꜣ ḏt(?) nb nḥḥ* 'Osiris, Ruler of eternal time(?), Lord of eternity'; 9) (human-headed) *ꜣst wrt* 'Isis the great'; 10) (human-headed) 'Nephthys'; 11) (falcon-headed) 'Horus'.
In the adjoining scene *wsir sš nsw mꜣꜥ mr.f imy-r pr n niwt rst ḏḥwtḥḥtp* 'Osiris, true scribe of the king whom he loves, steward of the Southern City, Dhutihotpe' raises his arms to three deities: Isis', 'Horus, son of Isis' and 'Imset Osiris, Lord of eternity'.

76 C. Leitz, *Lexikon der ägyptischen Götter und Götterbezeichnungen*, 2002, II, p. 111.

77 Followed by a horizontal line (cf. col. 203).

78 Written *š* for *k*.

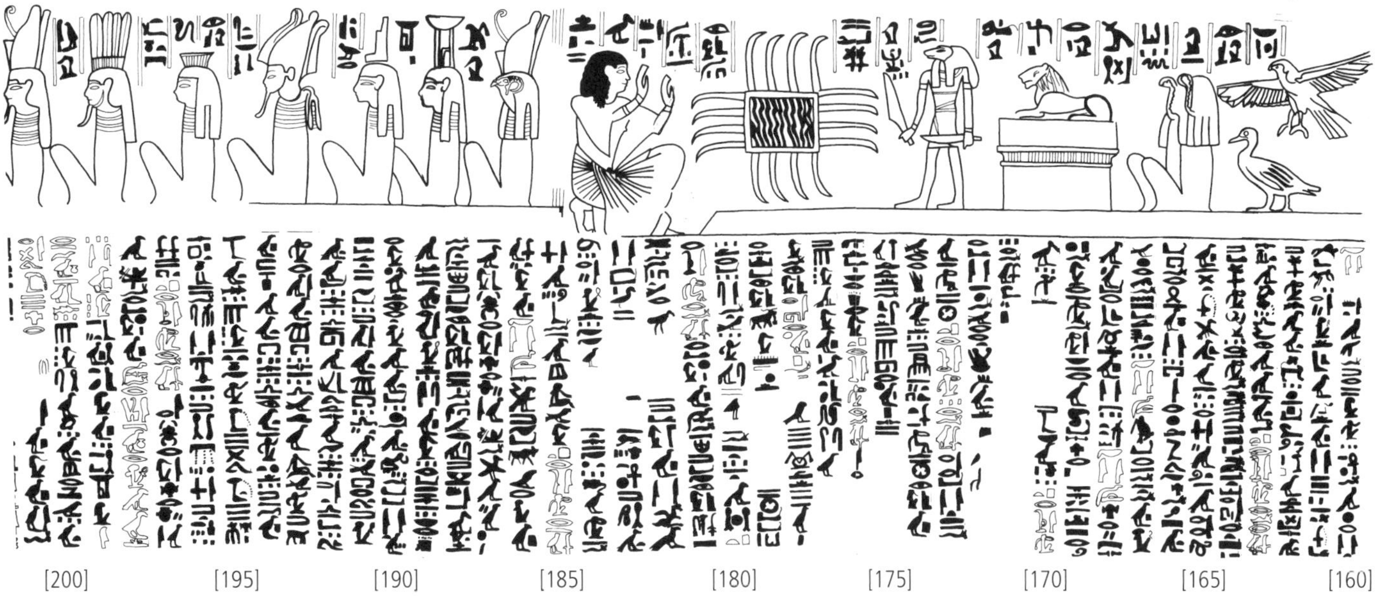

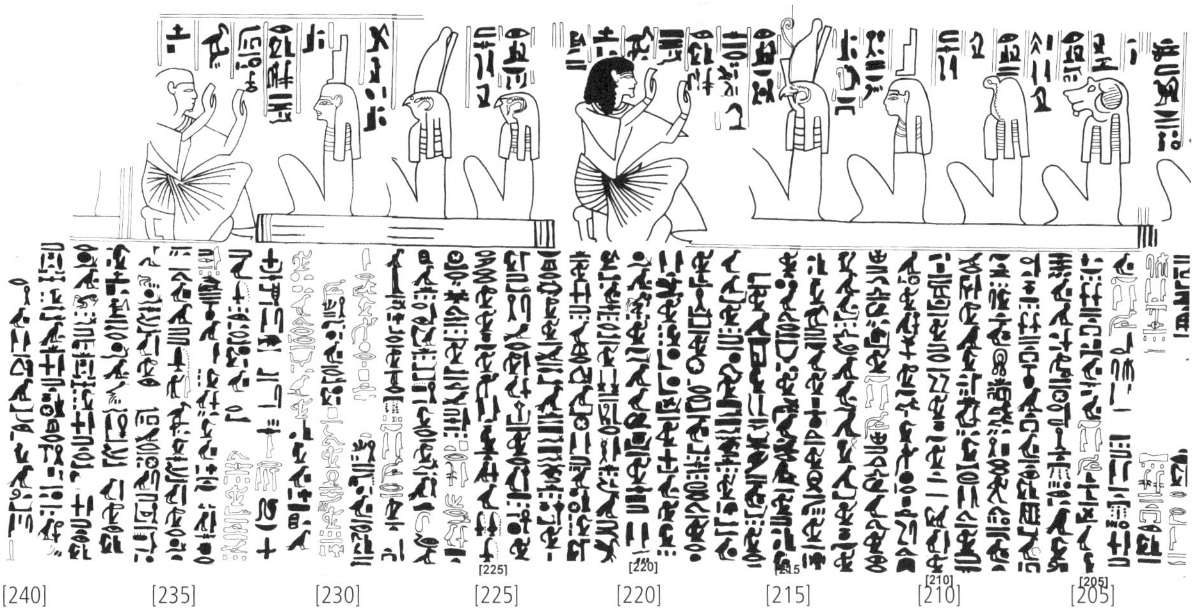

Figs. 23-24.
Section B cols. [160]-[240]

Behind the figure of Dhutihotpe there is a double line separating this scene from the next, and it would seem that another squatting deity was again the object of the tomb-owner's attention. The text of Spell 20 concludes at the end of our sheet, but it was evidently followed by another. In view of the appearance of Section C (see below) the spell must have been a different one, either not copied by Hay or now missing.

Spell 17 (continued)

[160] '*Otherwise said*: (It is the one) whose skin is human, who lives by slaughtering, who is in charge of those windings of the Lake of Fire, who swallows corpses,[79] who snatches hearts, who inflicts injury unseen.
Who is he? 'Swallower of Millions' is his name, and he is in the Lake of Wenet. Now as for that Lake **[165]** of Fire, it is what is between Naref and the House of the Entourage. As for anyone who treads on it, beware lest he falls to the knives. *Otherwise said*: Baby[80] is his name. He is the guardian to this interior of the West. *Otherwise said*: 'He who is over his affairs' is his name.

79 Copied as a ceremonial bed rather than Gardiner A14.

O Lord of terror who is at the head of the Two Lands, Lord of blood,[81] [whose slaughter-blocks] **[170]** are fresh, [who lives on] entrails.
Who is he? He is the heart [of Osiris...].
To whom was given the Wereret-crown and joy [in] Heracleopolis.
Who is he? As for him who was given the Wereret-crown and joy in Heracleopolis, he is Osiris.
[175] To whom was entrusted rulership among the gods on the day when [the Two Lands were] united [... in] the presence of the Lord of All.
Who is he? As for [him to whom was entrusted rulership] among the gods, he is Horus son of Isis, who was made ruler [in the place of] his father Osiris. *As for that day of* [uniting] the Two Lands, it is the union of the Two Lands at the burial of Osiris.
Potent ram [who is in] Heracleopolis who gives goodwill **[180]** and who drives off wrong-doers, to whom the ways of eternity are shown.
Who is he? He is Ra himself.
Save Osiris, true scribe of the king whom he loves, great steward, Dhuti[hotpe], justified from that god who steals souls, [who laps up corruption], who lives on what is putrid, who is in charge of darkness, [who is immersed in] gloom, of whom those who are among the languid ones **[185]** are afraid.
Who is he? He is Seth. *Otherwise said*: He is the great Wild Bull of Geb.
O Khepri in the midst of your sacred bark, primeval one whose body is eternity. Save Osiris true scribe of the king whom he loves, great steward, leader of festivals of Amun, Dhutihotpe from those who are in charge of those who are to be examined, to whom the Lord of All **[190]** has given the power to guard against his enemies, who put knives into the slaughter-houses, who do not walk away from their guardianship; their knives shall not cut into me, I shall not enter their slaughter-houses, I shall not die inside their fishtraps,[82] no harm shall be done to me by those **[195]** whom the gods detest, for I am pure, having passed pure on the Milky Way, one to whom has been brought a supper of the faience which is in the Tjenenet-shrine.
What does it mean? As for Khepri in the midst of his bark, he is Ra *himself. As for those who are in charge of those who are to be examined* they are the two baboons Isis and Nephthys. **[200]** *As for those things which* the gods *detest* they are excrement and lies. As for him who passed pure on [the Milky Way] he is Anubis who is behind the chest[83] [which contains the entrails of] Osiris. *As for him to whom has been given a supper [of faience which is in the Tje]nenet-shrine* he is Osiris. *Otherwise said*: As for the supper of faience which is in **[205]** the Tjenenet-shrine, it is sky and earth. *Otherwise said*: It means that Shu hammered out the lands in Heracleopolis. As for faience, it is the eye of Horus. As for the Tjenenet-shrine it is the tomb of Osiris. How well built is your house, O Atum![84] How well founded is (your) room, O Double Lion! Run quickly to this! If Horus be respected, Seth will be divine, and vice versa. I have come from this land **[210]**, I have used my legs, for I am Atum. I am in my town. Get back,[85] O lion, bright of mouth, shining of skin(?). Retreat because of my strength. *Otherwise said*: Retreat, you who attack me, O you who guard without being seen, do not guard me, for I am **[215]** Isis. You found me when I had disarranged the hair of my face and my brow was disordered. I have become pregnant as Isis, I have conceived as Nephthys. She drives off those who would disturb(?)[86] me; the fear of me follows after me, the awe of me is before me. Millions[87] bend their arms to me. People serve me; the associates of **[220]**

80 Written with the white crown on a standard, followed by an arm with a stick, cf. G. Lapp, *Totenbuch Spruch 17*, 2006, p. 260/261a.
81 The hieroglyph in the Hay MSS is unmistakenly Gardiner signlist N30. Parallel texts have *nb ḏšrw wꜣd nmwt* (cf. Lapp, *Totenbuch Spruch 17*, 2006, 264/265a).
82 As copied and probably written on the wall this appears to be a misreading of *ḥꜣdw*, the *ḥꜣ* having been mistaken for *smꜣ*, cf. a parallel in pBM 10793: P. Munro, *Der Totenbuch-Papyrus des Hohenpriesters Pa-nedjem II*, 1996, pl. 10, l. 1, cf. also G. Lapp, *Totenbuch Spruch 17*, 2006, 306/307d. These variants suggest that the word was re-interpreted as *smꜣwt.sn*, 'collecting points(?)', cf. col. 207 (=Lapp, 306-7d).
83 Horizontal line copied for *f*.
84 *mr* appears to be copied for *tm*.
85 Note the strange writing determined with F10 and A2 and the first sign almost like *ẖꜣ*.
86 *ẖnnw*.
87 In the Hay MSS the hieroglyph for *ḥḥ* (Gardiner C11) has been distorted, as has the writing of *rmnw*.

my enemies are destroyed for me; the grey-haired ones uncover their arms to me; the companions give sweets to me; those who are in Kheraha and those who are in Heliopolis create things for me. Every god is afraid of me because of the size and greatness of the awe of my protection of the god from him who would vilify him. A ray(?) glitters[88] for me, I live **[225]** as I wish, for I am Wadjet the Lady of flames, and few of them ascend to me.
What does it mean? 'Secret of shape, the arms of Hemen' is the name of the fish-trap. 'He who sees what he brings by hand' is the name of the storm-cloud. *Otherwise said*: *The name* of kettle(?)[89]
As for the lion whose mouth is bright and whose ... is shining, he is the phallus of Osiris. **[230]** [*Otherwise*] *said: he is the phallus of Ra. As for my having disarranged the hair of my face and having disordered my brow,* it means that Isis was in the sanctuary of Sokar[90] and she rubbed her hair. *As for Wadjet,* Lady of flames, she is the Eye of Ra. *As for few of them ascend to me',* it means that the companions of Seth approach her, for **[235]** what is near her is burning.'

This is the end of the spell itself, and the text continues straight on to Spell 20:

'O Thoth, you who justified (Osiris) against his enemies, justify Osiris great steward in the (Southern) city, leader of festivals of Amun-Ra Dhutihotpe, justified against his enemies as you justified Osiris against his enemies in front of the tribunal in which is Ra and in which is Osiris at the great tribunal which is in Heliopolis on that night of nocturnal matters **[240]** on that night of battle (against) those who rebelled.'

The complete Spell 20 is considerably longer, and it would seem to have continued here as well as under the part of the vignette above which was also omitted in Hay's tracings.

Section C

In this section of text the hieroglyphs are once more to be read from left to right. The first column of the tracings [241] contains the end of a Spell (see below), whereas cols. [242]-[256] are taken up by Spell 100 with instructions for use. After a declaration in cols. [257]-[260], Spell 101 begins at the top of col. [261] and concludes at the bottom of col. [280].
There are only two vignettes in this section of the text, some of the columns of texts taking up the full height of the register. Above Spell 101 we find a representation of Thoth with a large scribe's palette facing figure(s) now destroyed under the horizontal band of the sky. On the left above Spell 100 the tomb-owner stands with a cloth in his hand watching a boat sailing on a similar sky-line. The former could be seen as an illustration to Spell 94 which concerns Thoth presenting a water-pot and palette to the deceased.

Spell 100
[242] 'The Book of making a Spirit Worthy and *causing [it to go aboard] the Bark of Ra with those who are in his suite. Words to be recited by* Osiris, true scribe of the king whom he loves, great steward of the Southern City, overseer of the treasury of Amun-Ra, overseer of the two granaries of the North and the South, leader of festivals of all the gods of Thebes Dhutihotpe, justified.

88 Parallels have *sti* (Gardiner F29), but the hieroglyph copy looks rather like *nḏ*.

89 Perhaps Gardiner T34, *tnmt* (*Wb* V, 381,8), cf. G. Lapp, *Totenbuch Spruch 17*, 2006, 332/33b.

90 *sštꜣ*, cf. G. Lapp, *Totenbuch Spruch 17*, 2006, p. 363 n. 336,1.

He says: I have ferried over the phoenix to the East **[245]**, Osiris to Busiris, I have thrown open the holes of Hapi, I have cleared the paths of the sun-disc, I have dragged Sokar on his sledge, I have made the Great One in (her) moment, I have sung the praise of the sun-disc, I have united those who are among the adoring baboons, I have acted as second to Isis, I have strengthened her spirits, I have knotted the rope, I have driven off *Apopis*, I have driven off his (movements), Ra **[250]** has given me his arms, and (his) crew will not drive me away. If I be strong, the sacred eye will be strong and if the sacred eye be strong, I will be strong. As for him who shall hold back the prince Osiris, true scribe of the king whom he loves, great steward of the Southern City, overseer of the treasury of the Lord of the Two Lands, overseer of the granaries, leader of festivals of Amun-Ra Dhutihotpe from the sacred bark of Ra, he shall be held back from the **[255]** egg[91] and the abdu-fish.
To be recited over this drawing in writing which should be written on a clean blank scroll with powder of green glaze mixed with water of myrrh. To be placed on the spirit on his breast without [letting] it [touch] his flesh. He can go aboard the Bark of Ra, and Thoth will take count of him in coming and going.'

Following on from the conclusion of this spell is a declaration on behalf of the tomb-owner. This is a spell from BoD 129, a variant of spell 100:

'I am a spirit who raises up the *djed*-pillar, who establishes [the *tit*-knot] to sail with Ra in every place I wish, Osiris true scribe **[260]** of the king whom he loves, great steward of the Southern City, overseer of the treasury of the Lord of the Two Lands, overseer of the two granaries of the North and the South, leader of festivals of Amun-Ra Dhutihotpe.'

Spell 101
'The book of understanding (or: conjuring) the words of the place of embalming, a spell of the detestation of the chest, being what a father gives to his son.[92]
Words to be recited by Osiris true royal scribe of the king whom he loves, great steward of Amun, overseer of the treasury of the Lord of the Two Lands, leader of festivals of Amun-Ra in [Karnak] Dhutihotpe. He said: O you who are missing going out from the waters and climb(?) on the stern of your boat. May you proceed to the place where you were yesterday. You have included on **[265]** the stern of your boat the one greatly praised by the Lord of the Two Lands, true scribe of the king whom he loves, great steward of the Southern City, overseer of the treasury of the Lord of the Two Lands, leader of festivals of Amun-Ra in Karnak Dhutihotpe, justified, a worthy spirit, in your crew.
O Ra in this your name of Ra! If you pass by this sacred eye **[270]** of seven cubits its pupil of three cubits, you will make hale Osiris true scribe of the king whom he loves, great steward of the Lord of the Two Lands, leader of festivals Dhutihotpe, justified. If he be hale, you will be hale.
O Ra, if you pass by those who are upside down you shall cause to stand up the royal scribe, steward Dhutihotpe, justified, a worthy spirit, on his feet. If he is hale, you will be hale.
O Ra in this your name of Ra! If the mysteries of the Underworld are opened to you to guide the hearts of your Ennead, then you shall give **[275]** the heart of Osiris Dhutihotpe to him, a worthy soul in the Underworld. If he be hale you are hale.

91 Two intrusive sign groups have been inserted in the middle of the word *swḥt*, a bird followed by the plural pronoun *sn*.

92 I am indebted to Rune Nyord for translating and commenting on this rubric: The rubric follows closely the parallel in G. Lapp, *The Papyrus of Nu*, 2006, pl. 78 (101,1), except for the following points: There seems to be no room for a feminine ending on the genitive adjective after *mḏꜣt*, and the following word is written *rꜥḳ* by metathesis from *ꜥrḳ*. Hay's drawing clearly has *pr-nfr*, "Perfect House/Place of Embalming" rather than *pr-ꜥnḫ*, "House of Life". The drawing apparently adds an *r* before *rꜣ*, an addition paralleled in *pJwjꜣ* (I. Munro, *Totenbuch-Handschriften der 18. Dynastie*, 1994, pl. 57, l. 408). Unlike pNu, our text has the indirect genitive between *rꜣ* and *bwt*. The traces of a square sign before *dd* is not found in the parallels but could be tentatively read as the preposition *m*, "being".

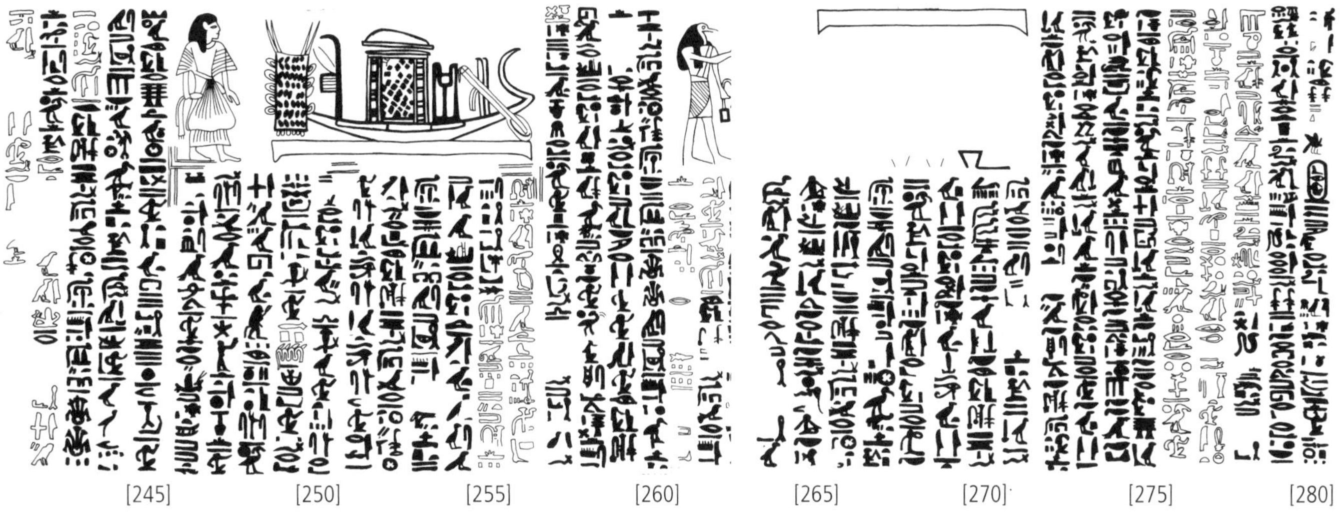

Figs. 25.
Section C cols. [241]-[280]

Your body, O Ra, is everlasting *by reason of the spell.*
To be recited over a strip of royal linen on which this spell has been written in dried myrrh. To be placed on the throat of the worthy spirit on the day of the burial. As for the one on whose throat this protective spell is placed, praises will be made for him as for the Ennead, he shall be united with the followers of Horus, the starry sky shall be made firm for him in the presence of him who is with Sothis. His corpse shall be a god, together with his relatives for ever, and a bush shall be planted for him by Menket. As for the one who did this for him**,** your back will go forth by day every day **[280]** from the West. It was the Majesty of Thoth who did this for the King of Upper and Lower Egypt Osiris, justified, so that the sunlight should shine on his corpse. Verified a million times.'

Col. [241], to the extreme left in Section C, contains hieroglyphs written in red ink. The lower half of the column was effaced, but the remaining signs were as follows:

These could perhaps be the end of Spell 134?

Additional vignettes

Three vignettes of the Book of the Dead were copied by Hay, without the columns of hieroglyphs which would presumably have been below.

Fig. 26 Hay MSS 29851, 101 (re-drawn by LM)

1) Hay MSS 29851, 101. Re-drawn from Hay and published in *Papyrus* 17/2, 1997/2, p. 15, fig. 5; omitting the tomb-owner in L. Manniche, *City of the Dead,* fig. 66.

The donkey and serpent is an illustration to Spell 40 which says; 'Get back, you swallower of an ass, whom he who is in the Netherworld detests.' The tomb-owner 'Osiris, royal scribe, Dhutihotpe' stands with a scribe's palette behind the serpent and donkey. The body of the quadruped is grey, the serpent being blue with black markings. The donkey has elongated proportions like those of a horse. The tail characteristic to a donkey was damaged, a fact that caused the present writer to mistake its identity in *City of the Dead* (as did indeed the *Top. Bibl*). In funerary papyri of the 21st dynasty the serpent is usually absent from this vignette.[93]
The figure of the tomb-owner measures 11.2 cm, the eye of 'Osiris' projecting slightly above this.

Fig. 27 Hay MSS 29851,100 (re-drawn by LM)

2) Hay MSS 29851,100. Re-drawn from Hay and published in *Papyrus* 1997/2, p. 15 fig. 6. This shows the tomb-owner raising a short stick towards a coiled up serpent. In the other hand he holds a scribe's palette and a yellow cloth. He is named as 'Osiris [true] scribe of the king whom he loves, steward Dhutihotpe'. The drawing may be seen as a vignette to Spell 39 which deals with repelling a serpent in the Underworld, except that this is habitually done with a knife or spear and not with a stick.[94]
The height of the register from base line to eye of 'Osiris' is 12.1 cm.

Fig. 28 Hay MSS 29851,102 (re-drawn by LM)

3) Hay MSS 29851,102. Published in *City of the Dead*, fig. 102; *Papyrus* 1997/2, p. 15, fig. 7. The vignette depicts two lions seated under a sun-disc on

93 Cf. R. Lucarelli, 'The vignette of ch. 40', 2007, pp.118ff.

pink horizon sand. The animals are yellow with red spots, their manes being red with black markings. A double lion is referred to in Spell 17 of the Book of the Dead (cf. our col. [210]).
The height of the register is 12 cm. The three vignettes could thus come from one and the same register of illustrations above a text that was not copied by Hay. They are too small to have belonged in a register with any of the other vignettes copied in sections A-B, but could possibly be fitted into a continuation of section C.

The three main sections of the Book of the Dead (A-C) vary in height and do not match one another:

Section	max. h. (incl borders)	h. excl. borders	h. of vignette
A	40.5 cm	34.5 cm	ca. 13 cm
B	40 cm	37 cm	ca. 15 cm
C	39.4 cm	33.7 cm	ca. 12 cm

The total widths of each section when arranged in one register are as follows (approximate measures based on each column of text + one dividing line being 2.5 cm in width):

A	150 cols. x 2.5 cm = 375 cm
B	81 cols x 2.5 cm = 202.5 cm
C	40 cols x 2.5 cm = 100 cm

The width of section A taking up 150 vertical columns of text and section B 81 cols, something is clearly missing in section C with its 40 columns plus additional vignettes, either because the wall was damaged, or, more likely, because some of Hay's tracings are lost (or were perhaps never carried out).

The choice of spells in TT A16

The spells included in the tomb are thus the following:
17 On the doctrine of Ra and Going forth by Day with vignettes (with vignette of the lions of the horizon from another part of the tomb copied separately)
20 Prayer to Thoth (part). Vignette(?) destroyed
23 Opening of the Mouth, no vignettes (space taken up by vignettes to spell 17)
100 On going into the bark of Ra, with vignette(?)
101 On protecting the bark of Ra. Vignette(?) partly destroyed
134 (? end)

Additional vignettes refer to other spells:
39 (repelling a serpent)[95]
40 serpent swallowing an ass
95 a goose depicted at the end of Spell 17 may refer to 'becoming a goose'

In representations of the Book of the Dead in the Theban tombs only a limited

94 J.F. Borghouts, *Book of the Dead (39). From Shouting to Structure*, 2007, p. 18.

95 For this chapter see now J. F. Borghouts, *Book of the Dead [39]. From Shouting to Structure*, 2007.

number of spells are included.[96] Spell 17 is the most frequently depicted (TT 219, 178, 296, 359, 360, 6, 158, 30, 10, 263 and C9). Spell 100 appears in TT 1 and 359 at Deir el-Medina, spell 23 being found in TT 359. Two of those included in TT A16 (spells 20 and 101) do not occur in any other tomb, nor do the vignettes of a serpent swallowing an ass and repelling a serpent which are only known from representations on papyrus.

In other Ramessid tombs, spells of the Book of the Dead may be arranged in two registers, separated by a horizontal band of text framed by horizontal lines. The Hay tracings do not show any such text, but only horizontal lines which may be interpreted as three lines (copied as double lines) framing two wider bands of colour (presumably red and black).

Position of the scenes

Neither Hay's team nor any of the other early travellers left any description of the tomb nor of its dimensions. The symmetrical representation of the tomb-owner in front of Osiris in its stela-shaped frame is around 100 cm wide and would fill the width of a narrow wall on its own with additional decoration below.

Sections A and B of the Book of the Dead both have neat right borders and the texts begin/end here, both being written with the signs facing right, but section B to be read in the opposite direction. All the vignettes show the tomb-owner facing right and the deities in the opposite direction. On examining the long section A (as joined by the author from Hay's loose sheets), there appears to be few places between vignettes where a vertical cut would not do some damage to the columns of text below. However, the 159 columns of section A (ca. 375 cm) may have spread over two adjoining walls. The only likely cut (change of wall) would appear to be between cols. 94 and 95 (in the middle of one of the sheets of tracing paper), the following cols. 95-159 (65 cols.) x 2.5 cm making a wall ca. 162 cm wide. Cols. 1-94 alone would take up some 235 cm plus a section where a sheet appears to be missing from the Hay MSS. Judging from the position of the vignettes and text, section B appears unlikely to have been broken up, suggesting a wall of just over 200 cm in width leaving the incomplete scene with the tomb-owner and bouquet for the right wall, which would then include the figure of Osiris appropriately seated with his back to the rear (west) wall. The figure of the tomb-owner, though rather similar to those on the stela, is slightly larger and thus probably does not belong immediately next to it.

96 M. Saleh, *Darstellungen des Totengerichts in den thebanischen Beamtengräbern des Neuen Reiches,* 1984.

TT A17

According to a sheet preceding folio 140 of Hay MSS 29851, tomb no. A 17 was 'a tomb opened by me near Piccinini's house, but covered before the colours were noted.' In MSS 29816,189 verso, however, he says that the tomb had been opened by Piccinini. Be this as it may, it was entered by E. Naville later in the century, for in his *Inscription historique de Pinodjem III*, published in 1883, he gives part of the text of one of the walls (p. 6, n. 3). The tomb, says the author, was a painted tomb at Draʿ abu el-Nagaʿ.
Four fragments of the wall-decoration have survived in museums. One (Fragment A) was bought on the art market in Cairo in 1910 for the Ny Carlsberg Glyptotek in Copenhagen. Three others (Fragments B, C, D) were acquired by the Field Museum, Chicago, having been presented to the museum by Edward B. Ayer in 1908. Some of these fragments have already been published by the present writer (see below).

The owner of the tomb and his relatives

TT A17 belonged to Userhet, chief of the measurers of granary of the estate of Amun in the reign of Ramesses III.[97] This exact date is indicated by the cartouche of that king on a painted stela in the tomb and on a stand depicted on Fragment A. According to Naville, the name of this king could be seen several times on the walls of the tomb.
Userhet's title is written as follows: *ḥri ḫꜣi*[98] *n tꜣ šnwty pr imn.*
Thanks to the note made by Naville we are informed that Userhet's father was a certain Pentawer, also chief of the measurers of the granary in the estate of Amun. It is the combination of the names of father and son, as well as their title, which enables us to link the Chicago fragments with this tomb. Fragment C depicts Pentawer himself, but the affiliation no longer exists. He is shown next to his wife, presumably Userhet's mother, who was songstress of Amun. Her name was on part of the fragment which has broken off.
Userhet's wife is depicted twice in the tomb as recorded in the Hay MSS. She too was a *šmʿyt n imn* 'songstress of Amun' and was called Hathor.

Naville provides us with the name of a son of Userhet, Dhutimes, who was *sš n tꜣ ḥwt wsirmꜣʿtrʿ mri imn m pr imn* 'scribe of the mansion of Usirmara, beloved of Amun in the estate of Amun.' A further relative depicted (Fragment B) was 'her daughter, his beloved *(sic!)*, songstress of Amun...' The name is indistinct, but most of the female determinative remains. The lady is seated next to Userhet himself.

97 Kampp, p. 616 also suggested 20**th** dynasty.
98 The hieroglyph above the arm with stick was copied identically in the two instances where the title occurs as ⸗. The granary hieroglyph shows the double granary (not available in the hieroglyphic font used here).

Fig. 29 Hay MSS 29851,146-50 (re-drawn by LM)

The decoration of the tomb

Scene A
Adoration of the Theban Triad

Hay MSS 29851,146-50. Re-drawn by the present writer for *Papyrus* 17/2, 1997, p. 14, fig. 3.

The representation showing Userhet and his wife adoring the Theban Triad undoubtedly came from an upper register of a wall in the tomb. The uneven upper line suggests an equally uneven ceiling. Since the feathers of Amun project above this line, it remains a possibility that an upper border framed the scene. The height of the register, measured from the base line to the tip of the feathers of Amun, is 51 cm.
An offering table with loaves, vegetables and flowers separates the couple (facing right) from the deities. Hathor, wife of the tomb-owner, shakes a sistrum, and we are to imagine the couple singing the praise of the Triad as the text above indicates:

←

rdit i͗ꜣw n i͗mn-rꜥ nsw nṯrw sn tꜣ n ḥr.f nfr di.f ṯꜣw kbḥ n kꜣ n wsir ḥri ḫꜣyw n tꜥ šnwty
pr i͗mn wsrḥꜣt snt.f mrt.f nbt pr šmꜥyt n i͗mn ḥthr mꜣꜥt ḫrw

'Giving praise to Amun-Ra, king of the gods; kissing the ground to his beautiful face that he may give bread, breath and cool water to the ka of the chief measurer of grain in the granary of the estate of Amun Userhet (and) his beloved wife, mistress of the house, songstress of Amun, Hathor, justified.'
Amun holds a papyrus umbel and *was*-sceptre in one hand and *ankh* in the other. He is identified as *i͗mn-rꜥ nsw nṯrw nb pt ḥkꜣ wꜣst nṯr ꜥꜣ ḥri-tp psḏt nṯrw* 'Amun-Ra, king of the gods, lord of the sky, ruler of Thebes, great god, chief of the Ennead.' Behind him, Mut acknowledges the adoration with one hand raised: *mwt nbt pt ḥnwt nṯrwt* 'Mut, lady of the sky, mistress of the godesses' The scene concluded with *ḫnsw m wꜣst nfrḥtp nṯr ꜥꜣ nb pt* 'Khonsu-in-Thebes-Neferhotep, great god, lord of the sky.' [99]

99 For Khonsu-in-Thebes-Neferhotep see now C. Leitz, *Lexikon* V, 2002, pp. 764-5.

Fig. 30 Hay MSS 19851,140-145
(re-drawn by LM)

Scene B
Adoration of Osiris and Hathor

Hay MSS 29851,140-45.

The height of this register is ca. 52 cm to the extreme right, slightly less to the left; the width of the scene, measured from the right extremity to the centre of the bouquet behind the tomb-owner's wife, is ca. 93 cm. To the left the representation continued in another scene (Scene C, see below).
The couple is here shown in adoration of Osiris and Hathor. Userhet presents incense and water while Hathor holds sistrum and papyrus umbel in one hand and a slender jar in the other. Two offering tables in front of them are laden with loaves, unguent(?) jars, fowl and flowers. The accompanying text above runs as follows:

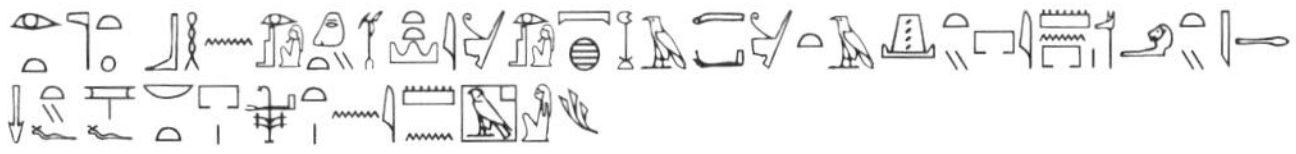

ỉrt sntr kbḥ n wsỉr ḫnty ỉmntt ỉn wsỉr ḥrỉ ḫ3ỉ n t3 šnwty pr ỉmn wsrḥ3t m3ᶜ ḫrw
snt.f mr.f nbt pr šmᶜyt n ỉmn ḥwtḥr

'Performing (the act of giving) incense and cool[100] water to Osiris, foremost of the West by Osiris, chief measurer of grain in the granary of the estate of Amun Userhet,[101] justified, (and) his beloved wife, mistress of the house, songstress of Amun, Hathor.'

The deities are positioned in an ornate naos, supported by two floral columns. They are accompanied by the following legend  *dd mdw n wsỉr nb*[102] *nḥḥ ḥk3 ḏt* 'Words spoken by Osiris, lord of eternal time, ruler of eternity', and  *ḥwtḥr nbt (t3) ḏsr ḥnwt nṯrw nbw* 'Hathor, lady of (ta)-Djeser, mistress of all the gods.'

100 The jar was left out.
101 Traces of the hieroglyph of a man(?) to the right of the oar.
102 Copied as *nbt*. (This is very common).

Fragment A

Fragment B

Fragment C

Figs. 31-33 Chicago

Scene C
Banquet

Hay MSS 29851, 140, 145; Chicago Field Museum nos. 105217-19.

The banquet scene adjoins Scene B to the left, as is apparent on Hay's tracings. It would seem that the remaining tracings by Hay's artists have now been lost, for the existing sheets finish abruptly half way through the seated figure of Hathor, wife of the tomb-owner, identified by the hieroglyphs [hieroglyphs]. However, two or three of the fragments now in Chicago would fit into this register which in the Hay tracings is to the left just under 52 cm high. The height of the registers in fragments A and B is about 51 cm, and the figures here are also facing left as in the Hay tracing. It remains a strong possibility that Fragment C belongs here as well, since it shows a man presenting a jar to a seated person facing left, just as the other main participants in the scene are doing.

Fragment A: Chicago Field Museum no. 105219
Manniche, *City of the Dead*, fig. 68; *Papyrus* 17/2, 1997, p. 13, fig. 2.
H. 51 cm; w. 29.5 cm

The scene shows a man and a woman (the latter partly destroyed) seated before a table laden with lotus, papyrus and a climbing plant. The man is the tomb-owner himself [hieroglyphs] *...n tꜣ šnwty pr imn wsrḥꜣt mꜣꜥ ḫrw* '[chief measurer] of the granary of the estate of Amun Userhet, justified.' He wears an unguent cone with a lotus flower and holds a sceptre in one hand, the other touching the offerings. His companion is [hieroglyphs] *sꜣt.f mr.f šmꜥyt n imn[...]* 'her daughter whom he loves, songstress of Amun...' The name of the girl would take up just one 'square', but it cannot be read with certainty.
With the exception of the hieroglyphs, most of the picture appears to have been retouched in modern times.

Fragment B: Chicago Field Museum no. 105217
H. 51 cm; w. 30 cm

This shows a man with unguent cone and lotus flower perched on his wig. He holds a sceptre in one hand and with the other he acknowledges the presentation of offerings of a papyrus umbel with a climbing plant and a jar on a stand, presumably positioned under a table. A person censes to the man, but only the incense burner and his fingertips remain. The recipient is *...n tȝ šnwty pr imn pntȝwr mȝꜥ ḫrw* 'of the granary of the estate of Amun, Pentawer, justified.' He was joined by *ḥmt.f šmꜥyt imn...* 'his wife, songstress of Amun...' whose skirt can be seen on the right.
As it was the case with fragment B, this one has been subject to some restoration.

Fragment C: Chicago Field Museum no. 105218
H. 44 cm; w. 31.5 cm

This fragment would appear to belong in the register under discussion, since it shows a man facing a seated person of similar dimensions as those mentioned above. Between the two, there is a table with loaves and a papyrus plant with the climbing plant around its stem. Behind the servant a second plant can be seen, possibly trailing rather than climbing. This fragment has been even more awkwardly restored than the previous two.

In an attempt to relate the four available pieces of the representation from the register showing Scene C we should undoubtedly visualize a row of seated figures, facing left, with tables and servants in between. Only the position of the tomb-owner's wife as drawn by Hay is certain to be adjoining Scene B.

Userhet's parents sit together on fragment B, here separated from Userhet, his wife and step(?)daughter by a standing servant. Other persons could have been inserted with this latter. The representation of Hathor may be joined with fragment A showing Userhet and the (step?)daughter, but it is possible that there existed another picture of Userhet which adjoined the representation of Hathor, his wife. It remains a possibility that the tracing in the Hay MSS came to an end with the edge of the sheet of tracing paper for the very reason that the neighbouring scene had been cut from the wall already at this early date, and that the surface of the wall had been destroyed in the process. On the other hand, there is nothing to suggest that the fragments had been detached for eighty years or so before they appeared on the art market. A missing sheet of the Hay MSS could well have showed a tracing of one or several of the paintings on the detached fragments.
Fragment C may tentatively be positioned on the left, allowing for at least one seated person whose legs appear on the fragment.

Fig. 34 Hay MSS 29851,140, 145
(re-drawn by LM)

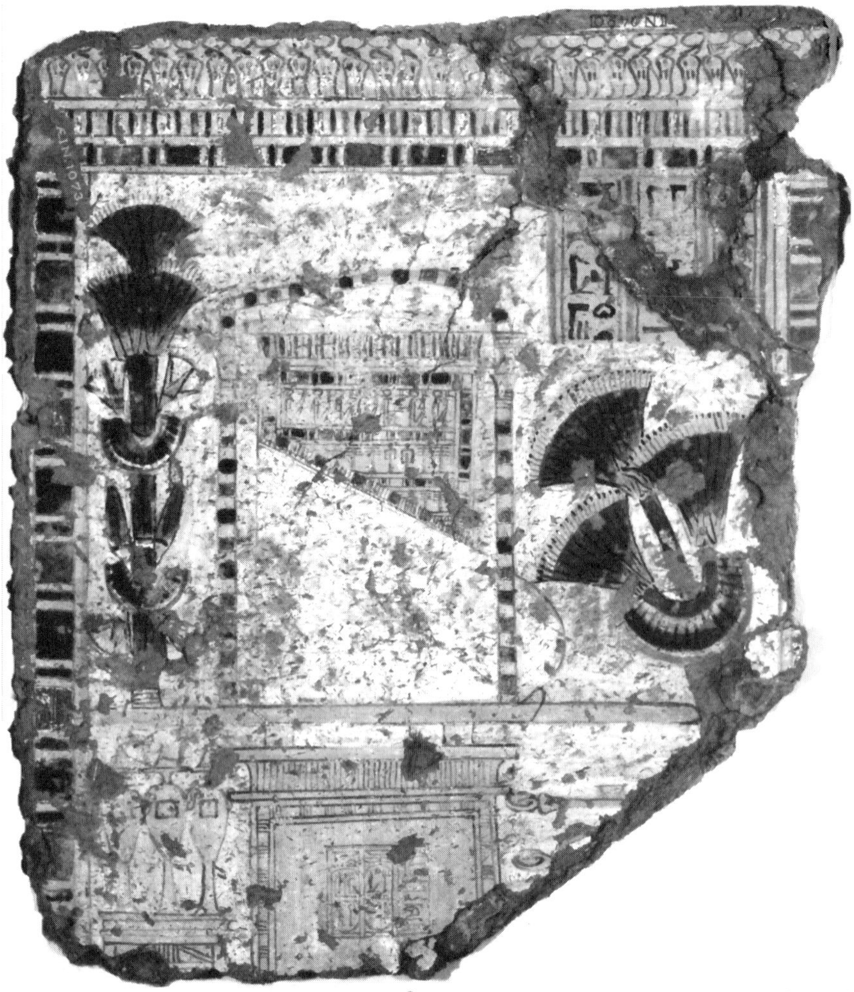

Fig. 35 Ny Carlsberg Glyptotek ÆIN 1073

Scene D
The Shrine of Amun-Ra Great-of-Awe

Fragment D: Ny Carlsberg Glyptotek ÆIN 1073
Manniche in *Göttinger Miszellen* 29, 1978, pp. 79-84; 58, 1982, pp. 49-51; *Papyrus* 1997/2, p. 12 fig. 1; M. Jørgensen, *Catalogue Egypt II (1550-1080 B.C.),* 2001, pp. 304-5. Inscription: Hay MSS 29816,198 verso [middle].
H. 45 cm; w.52 cm

The painting in Copenhagen which came on the art market soon after the turn of the 20th century, like the fragments now in Chicago, does not appear to have been subject to any of the restoration work which marred the others.
It represents a portable shrine, placed on a stand. The shrine itself was wrapped in a white shroud and sheltered by a light canopy. Inside would be the sacred image of the deity. A composite bouquet stands behind (to the left of) the shrine, while a larger bouquet leans towards it at the front. Both floral displays of three papyrus stems decorated with garlands, the one on the left having lotus flowers inserted. On the floor the priests have placed three tall *ḥs*-vases on a stand, each one having a square panel incised, no doubt intended for an inscription. The lower right corner of the fragment has been neatly cut away, but two arm-shaped censers can be seen here.

The support is decorated with a cavetto cornice and a panel at the side or front containing an inscription which reveals the identity of the deity and the dedicator of the monument:

nb t3wy wsr-m3ꜥt-rꜥ mry imn nb ḫ3w rꜥmss ḥk3 iwnw mry imn ꜥ3 šfyt

'The Lord of the Two Lands, Usirmaetra, beloved of Amun, Lord of Appearances Ramesses, Ruler of Heliopolis, beloved of Amun-Ra Great-of-Awe.'

The top right corner of the fragment contains an inscription in three columns painted on yellow (as opposed to the remaining background which is white):

i mn-rꜥ ꜥ3 šfyt nṯr ꜥ3 nb pt ḥk3 psḏt nṯrw

'A[mun-Ra] Great-[of-Awe]... Great God... Lord of the sky, Ruler of the Ennead.'

The representation of the chapel of Amun-Ra Great-of-Awe gives us some idea of the sphere of interests of our tomb-owner. The great god of Karnak showed himself in a variety of manifestations, and each one of these had not only his own cult and shrine, but also separate administration. According to Helck, the chapel of Amun-Ra Great-of-Awe was distinct from the chapel of Amun Great-of-Awe-in-the-Granary-of-Amun.[103] In that case we seem to have a conflict of interests in our tomb, for our chapel as represented on this fragment does not mention a connection with a granary, though the titles and functions of the tomb-owner strongly suggest that this is where his particular loyalties would have been (see further below). Amun was god of the living rather than a funerary deity. The greatest annual feast in the necropolis, the Feast of the Valley, may well have been held in his honour, but the occasion was one for those who had departed this world to join it again for a brief moment.[104] On the walls of the Ramessid tombs, Amun is referred to in the texts, but he is represented far less frequently than this would lead us to expect, and usually as part of the Theban Triad Amun, Mut and Khonsu. His sacred bark appears a few times as does a representation which is distinctly meant to be a statue of the god. If the god is present at all, he would be hidden inside a shrine as in the case of our fragment. The function of the god, and in this case his manifestation as Amun-Ra Great-of-Awe, be it the specific Amun of the granary or not, is thus to relate the tomb-owner to the world of the living and the ambience in which he spent his days on earth, and we must see it as one of the infrequent representations in a Ramessid tomb connected with the office of the tomb-owner.
A few other tombs at Thebes appear to have had a connection with Amun-(Ra) Great-of-Awe. Theban tomb no. 112, decorated in the 18th dynasty, was in the Ramessid period usurped by a man by the name of Aashefytemwese, meaning 'Great-of-Awe-in-Thebes', a name admirably suited for a person who was to become prophet *(ḥm nṯr)* in the service of the god. Another tomb, no. A23, belonged to a man by the name of Penaashefy ('The one belonging to Great-of-Awe-in-Thebes') who held the position of god's father *(it nṯr)* of Amun-Ra Great-of-Awe (for this tomb see below). It would be interesting in this context to consider whether it was possible to change one's name later in life. Kings

103 W. Helck, *Materialien zur Wirtschaftsgeschichte des Neuen Reiches,* 1960, p. 69 (no. 17).

104 For the Feast of the Valley see S. Schott, *Das schöne Fest vom Wüstentale,* 1953.

were obviously able to do so and adapt their names to their particular loyalties, but there seems to be little evidence for private individuals to have done the same, except perhaps during the Amarna Period. If this were indeed a possibility we could perhaps be faced with a kind of 'brotherhood' attached to this little known aspect of the deity.

Scene E
Painted stela

Hay MSS 29816,189 recto; cf. Naville, *loc. cit.*

It is thanks to Naville's footnote that we know that the scene in question was a 'painted' stela, and it is due to the copies of this stela and the text on the shrine on the same sheet in the Hay MSS that we can be confident that the two had an identical provenance.

The stela has a cavetto cornice and a frame of hieroglyphs inside which we find the round-topped stela. In the lunette is represented Ramesses III offering to the Theban Triad. The king, apparently offering a figurine of Maat, is named as *nṯr nfr nb t3wy wsim3ʿtrʿ mry imn* 'Good god, lord of the Two Lands, Usirmaetra-beloved-of-Amun'. An offering table with a jar and a flower separated him from Amun, Mut and Khonsu, the only inscription remaining being ... *n ḥk3 w3st* '[Amu]n ruler of Thebes'.

The text across the top is flanked by the two signs 'given life', separated by the text. Around the edge of the stela it runs as follows, beginning at the top, centre and going left:

←

s3 rʿ rʿmssw ḥk3 iwnw ʿnḫ nṯr nfr irt ḫt n it.f imn nsw bit nb t3wy wsrm3ʿtrʿ mry imn s3 rʿ nb ḫ3w rʿmssw ḥkʿ iwnw mry imn-rʿ

'Son of Ra, Ramesses Ruler-of-Heliopolis. May the good god live. Performing rituals for his father Amun (by) the King of Upper and Lower Egypt, Usirmaetra Beloved-of-Amun, son of Ra, lord of appearances, Ramesses Ruler-of-Thebes, beloved of Amun-Ra.'

Edge inscription going right:

→

nsw bit wsrm3ʿtrʿ mry imn ʿnḫ nṯr nfr imn-rʿ ms n mwt nbt pt nsw bit nb t3wy wsr3ʿ'trʿ mry imn

'King of Upper and Lower Egypt, Usirmaetra Beloved-of-Amun. May the good god live. [A verb omitted here? engendered? beloved?] by Amun-Ra, born of Mut mistress of the sky. (By) the Lord of the Two Lands, Usirmaetra Beloved-of-Amun' [here Hay adds 'as other side', i.e. 'son of Ra, Lord of appearances, Ramesses Ruler-of-Thebes, beloved of Amun-Ra.'

The nine horizontal lines of text on the stela give the following information. The hieroglyphs quoted here are those copied by Hay, with the variant readings by Naville indicated below.

Fig. 36 Hay MSS 29816,189 recto (re-drawn by LM)

ᶜnḫ nṯr nfr ḥᶜpy wr rnnw(t) ᶜ3t n kmt ir mnw m ib mrw n it.f imn nsw bit nb t3wy wsrm3ᶜtrᶜ mry imn s3 rᶜ nb ḫ3w rᶜmssw ḥk3 iwnw irtw.n.f šnwty ᶜ3t wrt ᶜḥᶜw st ḥr tkn r ḥrt n[105] *ᶜ3w n mrwt.f r nṯrw nbw di.f ᶜnḫ w3s nb snb nbt mi rᶜ ḏt*

'May the good god live (and) Hapy the great and Renenwetet great one of the Black Land, (the good god) who makes monuments with a loving heart for his father Amun, the King of Upper and Lower Egypt, Lord of the Two Lands, Usirmaetra beloved-of-Amun, son of Ra, Lord of appearances, Ramesses Ruler -of-Heliopolis. Making for him a very large granary, its heaps reaching to the sky, inasmuch as he is loved more than any other god, that he may give all life and dominion and all health like Ra for ever.'

The drawing of the stela in the Hay MSS is a hand copy, not a tracing. This may account for the differences in some of the writings compared with the rendering of the text by Naville, which is published in continuous horizontal lines of printed hieroglyphs.

105 The last sign of this line looks rather like the falcon.

We are here once more drawn into the special interests of our tomb-owner, for he has chosen to depict what was undoubtedly a real stela, erected by Ramesses III, near the very building which was the *raison d'être* of the monument: a huge granary-cum-shrine in the estate of Amun.
During the reign of Ramesses III granaries all over Egypt were registered and inspected, as recorded in the great Wilbour Papyrus, and if the walls of the buildings were found to have collapsed they were rebuilt. Although our text is not phrased as a 'restoration text', including words such as 'built anew' or similar, this could well be what is meant.

We can now consider Scenes D and E together. In one we have mention of a granary built for Amun-Ra by Ramesses III; in the other a representation of a shrine belonging to Amun-Ra Great-of-Awe, dedicated by the same king. Both scenes are on the wall(s) of the Theban tomb of a chief measurer of grain of the estate of Amun. This suggests that the actual building in question is the one listed as no. 17 by Helck[106] as the estate *(pr)* of Amun-Ra Great-of-Awe-in-the-granary-of-the-estate-of-Amun. Administrative documents of the Ramessid Period make reference to this granary: There is a record of 830 sacks of grain once being delivered from here.

Scene F
Opening of the Mouth

Hay MSS 29816,198 verso (upper).
The existence of such a scene in the tomb is suggested by a drawing above the copy of the inscription on the stand for the shrine copied by Hay. It shows a scroll of papyrus with the words  *ir wp(t) r irt.i* 'performing the opening of my(?) mouth and eye' written on it.[107] Hay calls it 'a papyrus read before the 2 mummy figs. as in another tomb", and he explicitly states that it was in the same tomb as the one with the stand. More than one mummy was depicted.

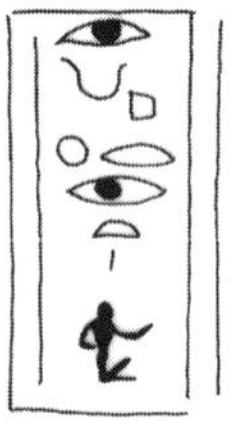

Fig. 37 Hay MSS 29816,198 verso (re-drawn by LM)

The scheme of decoration

The available tracings and fragments are far from sufficient to fill up the space of the walls in this tomb, and parts are obviously missing. The wall containing the adjoining scenes B and C is some 200 cm wide (unless the decoration continued on another wall). The deities face left and would thus naturally find their place on a left wall, or on the rear wall. The same may be said for fragment A. The fragment in the Glyptotek would best be placed on a right wall, the person presenting the large bouquet to the shrine being en route from the entrance of the tomb. Maybe the stela belonged here, too. This leaves the subject of the Opening of the Mouth unaccounted for. Many 18th-dynasty tombs have this subject on the right wall of a passage, but in theory it could be placed almost anywhere.[108]

106 *Materialien zur Wirtschaftsgeschichte des Neuen Reiches*, 1960, p. 69.
107 A parallel for the juxtaposition of mouth and eye may be found in A. de Buck, *The Egyptian Coffin Texts*, 1918, 7, 137c.
108 P. Barthelmess, *Die Übergang ins Jenseits in den thebanischen Beamtengräbern der Ramessidezeit*, 1992, Tafel I.

TT A23

This tomb was located at the inner end of a valley at Draʿ abu el-Nagaʿ, according to Champollion below TT A22 (his no. 49). This latter was 'on the side of a hill facing north, forming the south side of a small valley or inlet before arriving at the 3rd tomb (sc. TT A4) from Yanni's house.'[109] The tomb was thus in the part of the necropolis then known as Sheikh el-Atiyat.[110]

The owner was a man we mentioned under TT A17 above: Penaashefy, who held the office of 'god's father of Amun, god's father of Min, god's father of Amun-Ra Great-of-awe, overseer of the treasury'. He does not appear to be known from any other sources.

Among the early travellers only Champollion makes reference to the tomb (*Not. descr.* i, p. 541). The tomb was of the 'ordinary' plan and quite small. Most of the decoration remained sketched in red ink, few figures having received their colours. Almost all the columns for texts were left blank.

Among the subjects depicted were the following:

A adoration of Ra
B adoration of Osiris
C adoration of the Hathor cow
D agricultural scenes mostly destroyed.

The date of the tomb

Although agricultural scenes are predominantly a feature of tombs of the 18th dynasty, unless they pertain to the Hereafter, the name of the owner and the inclusion of adoration of Ra would point to a Ramessid date for this tomb. F. Kampp suggests a date in the 20th dynasty. Compared with the information from TT A16, mentioning the shrine of Amun-great-of-awe, this would seem likely.

TT A26

Compared with the 'lost' 18th-dynasty tomb no. A4 (Hay's no. 3) this one was, according to Hay, 'in the next valley or inlet towards the south, at the end and nearly at the top of the mountain at Draʿ abu el-Nagaʿ.[111] The name of the owner was not recorded, but it is undoubtedly a Ramessid tomb. Hay drew two cartouches ('the only two names I could find amongst the hieroglyphs'), but in his notebook he left them blank.

The decoration of the tomb

'The style is of the coarsest kind and clumsily but boldly drawn. The hieroglyphs are black and though daubed in show the usual facility with which they were executed' (MSS 29824,22).

109 For TT A22 see Hay MSS 29824,20 or diary 31054,136 and Manniche, *Lost Tombs*, 1988, pp. 54-5. There must be a writing error by Hay here, for the house must be that of Piccinini, not Yannis' house which was at Sheikh ʿabd el-Qurna. For the location of TT A4 see Manniche, *op. cit*, p. 5.

110 F. Kampp, *Die thebanische Nekropole*, p. 617 suggests between TT 142 and 16?

111 F. Kampp, *Die thebanische Nekropole*, p. 618 suggests a location near TT 163. This tomb, however, is to the *north* of TT 161 (and thus of Piccinini's house and the neighbourhood of TT A4). In the 'valley' to the south there was a tomb marked U on Wilkinson's map which bore the label 'tomb with a painted well.' This may – and may not – be TT A26.

Scene A

Hay MSS 29824, 21-2.

Due to the sketched nature of the one remaining illustration of the wall, Hay's description of the scene is included in full here:

'... a tomb without painting or sculpture in which is a pit that we descended perhaps 30 feet by a rope. The sides are rough and shapeless, but at the bottom is a small chamber where the figures at one end are curious.
The end wall we have drawn – the wall opposite the entrance is the following procession. 6 men carrying a boat with a gazelle's head – a sarcophagus in it with a hawk's head in the centre of the cabin[?]. In front of it are 4 hawks and then at the stern 3 oars much like we drew at Philae – a figure offering incense before it and preceded (by) standard bearers carrying the hawk. 2 foxes, a [here follows a sketch of a *tekenu*], the hawk and an ibis. The first hawk has the difference of wearing the [here follows a sketch of a headdress consisting of a disc and two tall feathers] cap. 4 figures carrying the 2 poles the end having feathers as at Medinet Habu in a procession. Between these poles are hawkheaded figures. 4 figures bear Mendes (*sic* – see below), black, he is preceded by a man carrying a lotus with the feather cap and a black fox headed figure beating the tambourine. To the whole procession[?] are many lines of hieroglyphs' (pp. 21-21 verso).

Fig. 38 Hay MSS 29824,22 [upper]

Fig. 39 Hay MSS 29824,21 verso [middle]

This wall opposite the entrance, described above, had a scene which was by *Top. Bibl.* classified as a 'funeral procession'.[112] It was, however, clearly of a more festive nature, as Hay had already noticed, with details similar to a representation in the second court at Medinet Habu.[113] Thanks to his very summary sketch and descriptions we can actually identify the subject as being the festivals of Sokar and Min, also depicted on the south wall of the second court of the temple of Ramesses III at Medinet Habu.[114]
The scene was depicted in one continuous register (although in the notebook drawn in two with the boat of Sokar above Min), the figures moving from left to right. Heading the procession is a man wearing the black mask of Anubis

112 p. 455.
113 *Medinet Habu* IV, 1940, pls. 218-26, esp. pls. 223 and 224; W. J. Murnane, *United with Eternity*, 1980, pp. 30ff, figs. 20, 21, 23.
114 See also G.A. Gaballa & K.A. Kitchen, 'The festival of Sokar', 1969.

and beating a large, round tambourine (also sketched at a larger scale on the page). This was the beginning of the scene, for Hay wrote 'the end' to the right of Anubis. He is followed by a group of four men carrying a statue of the black ithyphallic Min, in turn preceded by a man holding the emblem of the god: two tall feathers and a lotiform pole. Next come four men supporting two standards of Nefertum, the god of resurrection who also joined the procession at Medinet Habu. Between the poles of the two emblems are 'hawk-headed figures', a detail also apparent in the temple of Ramesses III.
Next we meet six men with standards. The emblems are as follows: ibis, hawk, *tekenu*, jackal, jackal, and hawk with double feathers. The procession concludes with the sacred bark of Sokar, carried by five men and preceded by a priest facing them.
In the Medinet Habu calendar[115] the festival of Sokar and Min took place during ten days from the third month of *akhet*, day 26. As in the mortuary temple of the king, the presence of this procession on the wall of the burial chamber must be seen in view of the part the deities played in the myths of resurrection and re-birth. The scene was accompanied by 'many lines of hieroglyphs'.

Scene B
Somewhere in the tomb 'the crocodile is represented - the sphinx, vulture and cows'. This entry in Hay's notebook follows the description of the procession and precedes mention of the ceiling, so presumably this was part of the wall-decoration, either on the right, left or front walls, or in a register below the procession.

Ceiling
'On the ceiling are the remains of boats in which is a globe which is the lion-headed deity & ibis adoring (p. 21 verso)'. Hay drew a sketch of the boat in question. This could be an illustration to Spell 62 of the Book of the Dead in which the deceased said: 'I am the one who journeys across the sky. I am Ra. I am the lion.'[116]

Fig. 40 Hay MSS 29824, 21 verso [lower]

Position of the scenes

It is of considerable interest that the scenes were placed in an underground chamber, no doubt the burial chamber, as, with the exception of the tombs at Deir el-Medina, these were generally left undecorated in private tombs of this period.[117] From a thematic point of view, the decoration of the ceiling, featuring the journey of the sun god, may be compared with the astronomical ceiling in the tomb of Senmut, setting the scene for the aspirations of the tomb-owner.
Being in honour of a funerary deity, the festival of Sokar was an appropriate topic for a burial chamber, here for the exclusive use of the owner of the tomb in his burial chamber.[118] Min, whose festival is at Medinet Habu also juxtaposed to the festival of Sokar, occurs less frequently in the tombs.[119]

115 *Medinet Habu* III, 1934, pl. 160.
116 The lion was connected with the course of the sun, see *LdÄ* III, col. 1081.
117 Exceptions from the 18th dynasty are TT 96B, 353.
118 The boat of Sokar is represented in a substantial number of Ramessid tombs (see index in *Top. Bibl.,* I,1, p. 489). The festival is mentioned in TT 192 and TT 50 from the end of the 18th dynasty.
119 TT 2 and 216 at Deir el-Medina; Min-Kamutef in TT 7, also at Deir el-Medina.

TT B1

This tomb was located in the area below the Assasif, by Lepsius (see below) referred to as 'el Barâba' (Arabic for 'old temple ruins'). According to Bonomi, 'el Birâbe' was the name for the brick arches above the Ramesseum, as it was indicated on Catherwood's map of Thebes drawn for Hay in MSS 28816,1.[120] It was, however, also applied to Bab el-Goria, a tomb in the Assasif 'where Yanni dug out some mummies, statues, boxes, papyri, bows, arrows, and all sorts of things found in tombs'.[121]

The only record of this tomb appears to be a reference in Lepsius MS 262 [middle and lower, No. 9].[122] He describes the tomb as being 'nahe unter den eigentlichen Assasif Gräbern, an einem tieferen Ort, genannt el Barâba.' It was a roughly finished tomb ('das Grab war nicht einmal abgeglättet an den Wänden, sondern die Gypslage nur über den roh abgehackten Fels gelegt, und oft schief und krumm').

The owner of the tomb

The owner was Mahuhy, who was a *wꜥb n imn m ipt swt* 'wab-priest of Amun in Karnak', the name of his father being Nedjem and that of his mother Tanekhenemhab.

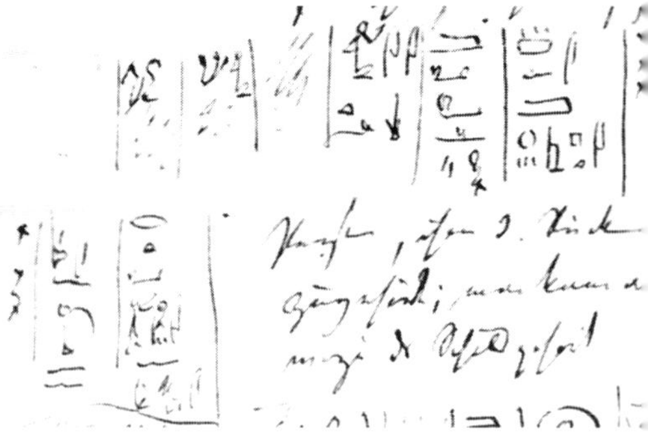

Fig. 41 Lepsius MS 262 [middle]

The decoration of the tomb

Tomb-owner praying before gate

Lepsius refers to a scene where the tomb-owner, followed by his wife, adores four gates with an inscription running from right to left in vertical columns ('Einmal bietet er vier Thore an, und scheint da zu heissen'):

rdit i3w n iry [sbḫt] in ḥri(?) wꜥb (n) imn m ipt-swt mꜥḥwḥy snt.f [...] mwt [...]

'Giving praise to (the [gate]-keeper by the head(?) *wab*-priest of Amun in Karnak, Mahuy (and) his wife... (and) [his] mother? [...]'

The couple would be facing left across to the gate-keeper. One would expect to find this scene in the upper register of a right wall of a small tomb.[123]

Tomb-owner adoring Amunet(?)

Lepsius continues to mention the tomb-owner praying before Amunet(?) 'with the lower Pschent'. Osing read this as Amun and the following signs as a possible abbreviation for 'd(or)t'. In view of Amunet being twice mentioned in the text (and not Amun) as the object of the adoration, it would seem better to read 'Amunet'. A pschent is the Greek vocalization for the double crown, but it is possible that Lepsius referred to the red crown as a 'lower (Egyptian) Pschent'. Amunet generally wears this red crown. Such one also features prominently in

120 This map is reproduced in D. Eigner, *Die monumentalen Grabbauten der Spätzeit in der thebanischen Nekropole* 1984, fig. 4. Birabi is no. 8. For Bonomi's notes see Newberry, 'Topographical notes on Western Thebes...', 1906, pp. 78-86. No. 58: 'El Birabe. The low walls in front of Piccinini's house extending to the cultivation.'

121 P. E. Newberry, *op. cit.*, no. 23, cf. no. 22.

122 I am indebted to J. Osing for implementing the decipherment of the scribblings of Lepsius.

123 Cf. above under TT A15.

124 *Top. Bibl.* I,2, p. 542 (40) in the Amduat.

125 *Top. Bibl.* I,2, p. 754 (8), paired with Selkis on door jambs.

the inscription in an uncertain context, maybe merely phonetic. It is the only occurrence of this goddess in a private tomb at Thebes, but she features in the tomb of Sethos I[124] and in a tomb of one of the sons of Ramesses III.[125]
Behind the tomb-owner there was another priest with his back to him, and, according to Lepsius, it is not possible to see to whom the inscription belongs:

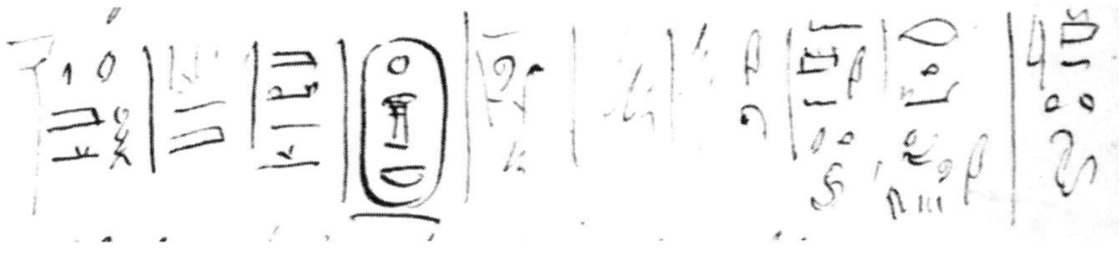

Fig. 42 Lepsius MSS 262 [lower]

rdit iʿw n imnt… i[n][126] *wʿb [mʿḥwḥy]] n(?) dšrt(?) ḏdnbrʿ mʿḥw… sꜣ nḏm*

'Giving praise to Amunet by the *wab*-priest [Mahuhy] to(?) the red crown (?) of Nebdjedra(?) Mahu[hy], son of Nedjem.'[127]

The context of this part of the inscription remains obscure. The cartouche as copied is unknown. The closest parallel would be Mentuhotpe Nebhepetra of the 11th dynasty. The cartouche must be part of a title. It may be of interest in this connection that a statue of Mahuhy's father was found at Deir el-Bahari (see below).

To the right is the beginning of another legend, written in the opposite direction, with the name of Amunet:

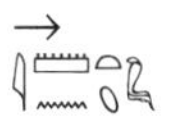

Based on this information we should visualise the tomb-owner facing right, adoring Amunet facing left. To the left behind the tomb-owner ('links hinter ihm') would be the priest. Lepsius places this scene 'elsewhere' in the tomb (compared to the previous one) ('ein andermal…)'.

Fig. 43 Lepsius MS 262 [lower right]

Scene referring to Ramesses III

Behind the priest just mentioned ('weiter hinten') the cartouche of Ramesses III could be seen, but the context was unclear to Lepsius. If represented near his name, the king would be facing right and thus be represented opposite the priest (unless another motif separated them). Be this as it may, the presence of the cartouche suggests a date for the tomb.

Further to the date of the tomb

Although we have no further information of the tomb itself, we are, however, able to follow up on Mahuhy's parentage in a block statue of his father Nedjem, a scribe, son of Bekenmut, with his wife Tanekhenemhab and Mahuhy, their son represented in relief on the sides. It was found by Naville at Deir el-Bahari and can be dated to the reigns of Merneptah and Ramesses III[128] The statue is now in the Metropolitan Museum of Art.[129]

126 Below the reed a curved line suggests and the beginning of the owner's titles.
127 Lepsius copied *ḥ*, but it must be *nḏm* – see further below.
128 E. Naville, *The XIth Dynasty Temple of Deir el-Bahari*, 1913, iii, pls. iv, [5], x [a], p. 7; J. Pijoan, *Summa artis,* 1945, iii, fig. 593; *Metropolitan Museum of Art Bulletin* (1907), p. 22; *Top. Bibl.* II, p. 381. F. Kampp, *op. cit.*, p. 618 dates our tomb to the reign of Ramesses III.
129 No. 06.1231.88.

TT C7

With this tomb we appear to move to another area of the necropolis, namely to Sheikh ᶜabd el-Qurna. Both Champollion and Rosellini gave it the number 27, their no. 28 being the lost 18th-dynasty tomb TT C6 which was to the east of TT 343, that is to say in the plain opposite the Ramesseum.[130] The tomb was apparently not visited by other scholars neither before nor since. No complete scenes were recorded, but a few inscriptions were copied and sketches made.

The owner of the tomb

This was a man called Horimosi (in the *Top. Bibl.* transcribed Harmosi) who was *ḥri s3wty pr ḥḏ m ḥwt nsw ḫr imnt w3st*, var. *ḥri s3wty pr ḥḏ nb t3wy* 'head custodian of the treasury of the king's mansion in western Thebes'. The king in question was Ramesses II.
The wife of the tomb-owner was Mutemwia. A son was a scribe called Kaemwaset.

The decoration of the tomb

According to Rosellini MSS 284, G36 the tomb was well painted, but all destroyed. Champollion, *Not. descr.* p. 517 was of a different opinion: 'La peinture en est assez negligée'. The tomb had two small rooms. As to the first we are informed about the decoration of the rear wall which was divided into three registers. The upper register had a double scene comprising adoration by the tomb-owner of the royal bark and the bark of Ptah-Sokar-Osiris. In the former scene Horimosi stands inside a building, adoring an ornate boat, which had at the stem and prow a head with an *atef*-crown:

Fig. 44 Champollion, *Not. descr.* p. 517

Champollion copied an inscription near this scene. It could have been written on the stand of the sacred boat as in a similar representation in TT A17 (see above). It took up the space of a square panel as follows

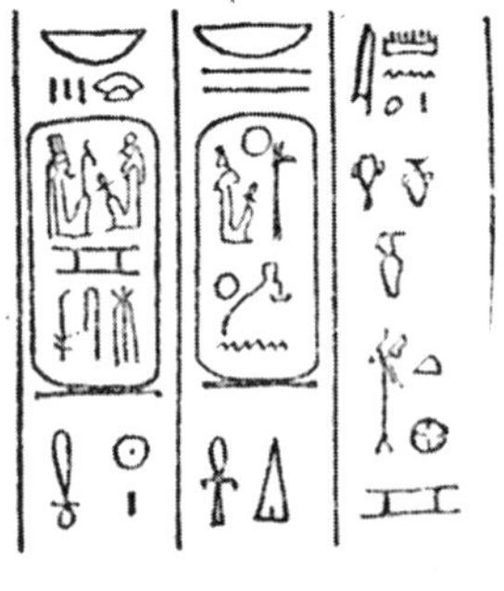

Fig. 45 Champollion, *Not. Descr.* p. 517

nb t3wy wsrm3ᶜtrᶜ stpnrᶜ nb ḫ3w rᶜmssw mry imn di ᶜnḫ mi rᶜ mry imn-rᶜ ḥri ib ḫnm-w3st

'Lord of the Two Lands, Usirmaetra-Setepnra, Lord of Appearances, Ramesses Beloved-of-Amun, beloved of Amun-Ra who is in United-with-Thebes (= the Ramesseum).'

130 F. Kampp, *Die thebanische Nekropole*, p. 620 also suggests a location to the east of TT 343.

The boat itself was 'without name'. No details are forthcoming about the neighbouring scene with the boat of Ptah-Sokar-Osiris.
The second register had a representation of a row of deceased kings and Horus *(sic!)*. This was probably Haremhab, who in official records was next in line. Champollion sketched their heads ('Horus' being 'the last'):

Fig. 46 Champollion, *Not. descr.*, p. 518

and gave their names in transcription, whereas Rosellini provided the cartouches with the names in hieroglyphs (omitting 'Horus'):

Fig. 47 Rosellini MSS 284, G36

Amenhotpe III Tuthmosis IV Amenhotpe II Tuthmosis III Tuthmosis II Tuthmosis I

The remaining part ('more than half') of the register was destroyed. From Rosellini's notes it would appear that the damaged part was to the right, i.e. where kings earlier than Tuthmosis I may have been depicted. We should expect to find at least Amenhotpe I, his mother queen Ahmosi Nefertere, and possibly also king Ahmosis. Facing them would perhaps be a picture of either the tomb-owner or his sovereign, adoring or offering to these kings of the 18th dynasty, as in other tombs, notably at Deir el-Medina.[131]
The third register would have been interesting to study, but we only have Champollion's brief description of it. It showed the pylon of a 'palace' with a statue of an ithyphallic(?) Amun and the boats arriving along the canal which was bordered by trees. We already met the combined representations of Sokar and Min, or Amon-Min/Kamutef in TT A26 above.
The second chamber opened to another room on the left. Its walls were covered in 'religious' scenes. In the 'frieze' Champollion copied the title of the tomb-owner

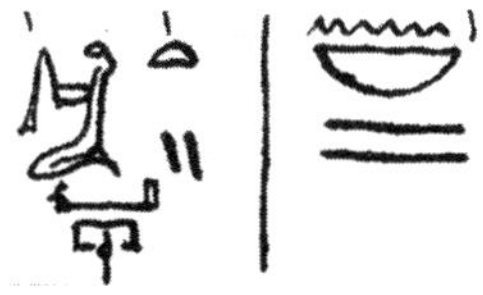

Fig. 48 Champollion, *Not. descr.*, p. 518

s3wty pr ḥḏ n nb t3wy

'custodian of the treasury of the Lord of the Two Lands'.

This differs from the one given in Champollion's heading to the paragraph. The latter was copied near a representation of the tomb-owner facing left.

131 See *Top. Bibl.* I,1, index 30 'deceased kings and/or queens'.

TT D2

This tomb was located 'below the hill', i.e. of Qurnet Muraʿi. It belonged to  Petersuemhebsed. A person of this name is known from a shabti in Leningrad State Hermitage Museum, no. 950.[132] His title here is 'servant', and the name is written in a slightly different way: . The name is also mentioned in a letter in Leiden, written in the reign of Ramesses II.[133]

One scene in the tomb, referred to by Wilkinson in MSS v.173 [bottom], contained a representation of Amenhotpe I and Ahmosi Nefertere, which would suggest a Ramessid date for the tomb.[134] However, this subject seems to have been continued beyond the Ramessid Period, cf. TT A18 below. Another scene showed Ptah-Sokari.

132 W. Golenischev, *Ermitage Imperial. Inventaire de la collection égyptienne*, 1891, p. 138.
133 J.J. Janssen, *Nine Letters from the Times of Ramses II*, 1960, (363,1).
134 *Sic* also, with a question mark, Kampp, *Die thebanische Nekropole*, p. 620.

Part II Post-Ramessid Tombs

TT A18, B3, C14

TT A18

This monument raises some interesting questions with regard to its date and the possible historical significance of its inscriptions.
Wilkinson (MSS v.150 [lower]) identifies the tomb as 'Piccinini's tomb', it being located near the house of this gentleman on the slopes of Draᶜ abu el-Nagaᶜ, in the vicinity of TT 161 (Hay MSS 29816, 136: 'at the back of Piccinini's house'; Hay MSS 29824,1 verso: 'Behind the Mummy Tomb' [sc. a mummy pit?]; Hay MSS 29824,1 verso: 'Behind Piccinini's house'.) In the Rosellini MSS it is said to be the 'tomba magazzino della nostra cucina'. Due to the Italian connection, it is to be expected that Rosellini would use the facilities of Piccinini. Thus the tomb must have been immediately adjacent to the old house of Piccinini. If used as a storeroom or larder, and hence exposed, it would probably not have survived well.
Hay described the wall-decoration in some detail (MSS 29824,1-2), including some sketches (MSS 29816,136-7), and Wilkinson copied a few inscriptions (MSS v.150-1) and drew one sketch (MSS v.170 [middle]). The expedition of Lepsius only copied a few names (MSS 428-9). The most extensive work is due to the combined efforts of Champollion and Rosellini who both included drawings in their publications. References have been made to these by more recent authors (see below under the individual scenes). The tomb itself was apparently not entered after the Franco-Tuscan expedition left it. On the basis of previous copies, some of the texts have recently been published by Karl Jansen-Winkeln.[135]

The owner of the tomb

 Amenemopet, the tomb-owner, held the following titles:
 *ḥm nṯr imn-rᶜ nsw nṯrw* 'prophet of Amun-Ra, King of the gods'
, var. 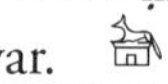 *ḥri sšt3* 'head of secrets'
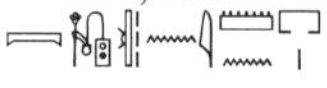 *ḥri sš mḏ3t n pr imn* 'chief document scribe of the estate of Amun'.

However, the *mḏ3t* scroll has also been read as *ḳd*,[136] a reading which also appears on items of funerary equipment probably from this tomb. In that case we may have an explanation for this tomb which is the sole, decorated Theban tomb from the 21st dynasty. If the tomb-owner was an outline draughtsman, and not only a literate bureaucrat, the temptation to design a funerary monument for himself must have been self-evident. Contemporary coffins provide ample proof of the still extant expertise in the field.

His father was Pa'ankhemdiamun. He had a son,  Djementef'ankh, whose title was 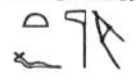 *it nṯr mry*, an abbreviated writing for *it nṯr mry nṯr* 'god's father, beloved of the god'. A 'son of his son', perhaps this one, was also called Amenmopet. He held the title of 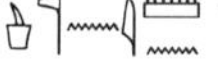 *it nṯr n imn* 'god's father of Amun', and he was also  *sš mḏ3wt* 'document scribe'.[137]
In addition, our tomb-owner had four daughters. We do not know their names, but their husbands are depicted on one of the walls of the tomb. They were

135 *Inschriften der Spätzeit. Teil I: Die 21. Dynastie*, 2007, pp. 218-20.
136 K. Jansen-Winkeln, *Inschriften der Spätzeit. Teil I*, 2007, pp. 218-20.
137 K. Jansen-Winkeln, *Inschriften der Spätzeit I*, 2007, p. 218 reads *sš ḳdwt*, adding *(sic)*. The sign is indistinct, written in a vertical position. See further below, p. 77 n. 160.

Nesamun[138] *ḥm nṯr n ỉmn sš ḥwt nṯr n pr ỉmn* 'prophet of Amun and scribe of the temple of Amun'; Khensmosi[139] *ỉt nṯr mry nṯr ḥry n šd n pr ỉmn* 'god's father, beloved of the god, head reader in the estate of Amun'; Pedekhons, 'god's father, beloved of the god, head reader'; and Ankhefkhons, *ḥsb ỉt n pr ỉmn* 'counter of grain in the estate of Amun'. The father of this latter person was a certain *ỉt nṯr mry (nṯr) ḥry … Imn* 'god's father, beloved of the god, head (of the kitchen of the estate of?) Amun' called Nakhtamun.

The name of the tomb-owner's wife is by *Top. Bibl.* given as Ankhenkhons, based on an entry in Lepsius MS 429:

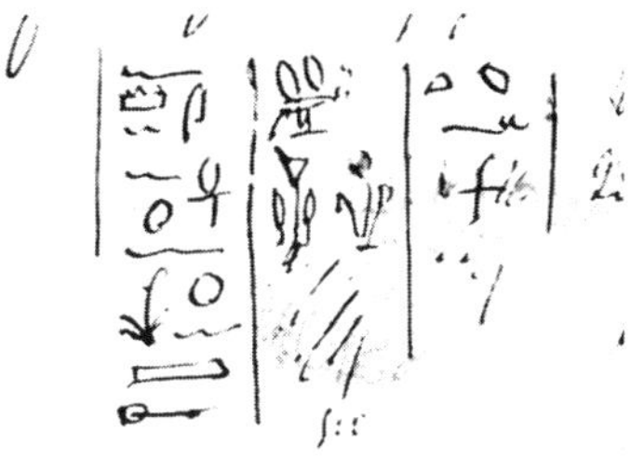

Fig. 49 Lepsius MS 429

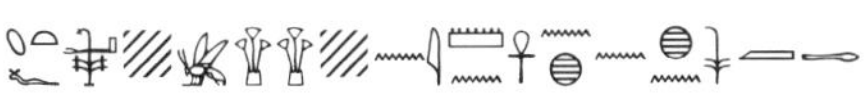

s3t.f šmᶜyt n …3ḫ-bit[140] *n Imn ᶜnḫnḫns m3ᶜ ḫrw*

'…(?) his daughter, songstress of … of Amun, Akhenkhons, justified.'

One of the sons-in-law is called Ankhefenkhons, but because of the title and the feminine ending this must be a different individual, not an erroneous copy.[141]

The date of the tomb

The *Top. Bibl.* dated the tomb to the Ramessid period. Some have been even more specific and suggested the reigns of Ramesses III and IV.[142] There are no Ramessid cartouches extant in the tomb, but the scenes copied by the early travellers would perhaps indicate such a date: representations of the deified king Amenhotpe I and his relatives [fig. 54 and 55]; extracts from funerary rites [fig. 53]; a 'rewarding' scene [fig. 51]; and even a 'weighing scene' mentioned by Hay. However, a close scrutiny of the inscriptions on the walls of the tomb suggests an alternative possibility.

The name of Amenemopet itself offers no clue, for it was a common name from the 18th dynasty and well into the Late Period. But most of the other persons depicted in the tomb have names some of which were perhaps in use under the Ramessid kings, but became even more popular during the following dynasties: Nesamun, Pedekhons and Khensmosi to mention those which can be read without ambiguity. The name of Pa[n]maᶜet which we also meet in the tomb (fig. 53), appears only in the Late Period, and Djementef'ankh occurs only from the 21st dynasty and onwards.

The writing of the names of Amenhotpe I differs from that in use during the king's life-time as well as in the reign of Amenhotpe III and during the course

138 Cf. *Top. Bibl.* I,2, p. 813; Hay MSS 29821,4: wooden stela of Nesamun, royal scribe, sealer of Amun-Ra, son of Panma'et. However, Nesamun was a fairly common name.

139 Cf. *Top. Bibl.* I,2, p. 637: coffin from Deir el-Bahari cache of a Khensmosi, scribe of the estate of Amun.

140 In Lepsius' hand, the two plants are not absolutely identical, cf. also K. Jansen-Winkeln, *Inschriften der Spätzeit I*, p.163 no. 1. The two plants may be a perverse writing of *3ḫ-bit,* Chemmis?

141 An ushabti box in Berlin (11987-9) combines the names of Ankhefenkhons + Khensmosi + Nesamun (*Top. Bibl.* I,2, p. 641).

142 E. Lüddekens, 'Untersuchungen über religiösen Gehalt, Sprache und Form der ägyptischen Totenklagen' 1943, p. 158.

of the 18th and 19th dynasties, when the cult of this king and his family, especially his mother Ahmosi Nefertere, climaxed. In our tomb additional signs are found inside the cartouches () and (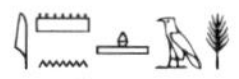[143]), and we seem to be presented with an epithet of the king not otherwise applied to him:  *dgi pȝ tȝ ꜥȝ.f* 'whose greatness the country beholds?'[144] followed *mri imn,* 'beloved of Amun'. These writings are indicative of a post Ramessid date (see further below).

In his dissertation on grave goods from the 3rd Intermediate Period, D. Aston briefly discussed the date of TT A18 suggesting, based on the names, a date after the Ramessid period. He has since elaborated on this and narrowed it down to ca. 1000-950 BC.[145] The work of van Walsem on contemporary coffins also suggests a mid or late 21st dynasty date for this tomb in that a coffin of this date can be related to the tomb-owner's son.[146]

A further indication that we have to consider activities in the tomb at a date later than the Ramessid kings comes from the notebooks of Wilkinson (MSS v.150-51). At the doorway of the tomb Wilkinson copied an inscription, reproduced in full below, p. 75, fig. 50), which includes the following two cartouches: () *(sic)* and ().
These were referred to in the footnotes of a work by an authority of the Third Intermediate Period,[147] but the evidence they provide was not discussed in that place in relation to the interesting information suggested in the funerary and rewarding scenes elsewhere in the tomb. The cartouches which are not juxtaposed in the manner of a full royal titulary appear to read 'Psusennes' and 'Hedjheka...ra'. In his work Kitchen does not commit himself to an interpretation of these data, except for making mention of Psusennes II (III?) rather than Psusennes I.
Subsequently, this inscription has been studied by A. Dodson in connection with the possible existence of a Psusennes III.[148] If Wilkinson's copy were correct, we would be faced with a royal name, Hedjheka...ra, not attested elsewhere. It is a king's prenomen, preceded by *nsw bit*. Kitchen takes the two catouches as referring to one king. If on the other hand Wilkinson miscopied one sign in a cartouche of which the lower part was already illegible, one cartouche could refer to Psusennes II, last king of the 21st dynasty, and the other to Sheshonk I, first king of the 22nd, whose prenomen was Hedjkheperra-setepenra, being copied for .[149] Dodson takes the inscription to be an official's graffito recording his services under two separate kings at the end of the 21st and the beginning of the 22nd dynasties. Hence he implies that the tomb was decorated at an earlier date (see further below).
Leaving this option aside for a moment, and working on the assumption that the cartouches are contemporary with the rest of the decoration of the tomb, we shall now turn to the remaining two pieces of evidence from the tomb which may provide confirmation of its place in time. In the 'rewarding scene' (fig. 51), neatly published by Rosellini, we meet Amenemopet and his relatives at a function which is presided over by a person identified  *it nṯr ḥm nṯr tpy n imn* 'god's father, first prophet of Amun.' The title and the beginning of the name continue behind his legs:  [gap?] ... *imy-r mšꜥ wr ḥȝwty...* a 'chief of the army, chief commander'. The bird following the latter title should probably read *wr*, the title being 'generalissimo', followed by

143 Copied as a papyrus (*wȝḏ*), see also below. The bird is indistinct.
144 Or possibly, following a suggestion by P. J. Frandsen, by emending to *dgi pȝ tȝ <m> ꜥȝ.f,* 'by whose greatness the country sees'. I am indebted to T. Moore for commenting on these epithets as found on contemporary coffins during the early stages of my work.
145 *The Shabti Box*, pp. 31 and 52; also book review in *JARCE* 28, 1991, pp. 233.
146 R. van Walsem, *The Coffin of Djedmonthuiufankh*, 1997, pp. 313-4.
147 K. Kitchen, *The Third Intermediate Period,* 1973, p. 12 n.46.
148 'An enigmatic cartouche', 1988, pp. 15-18; 'Psusennes II and Shoshenq', 1993, pp. 267-8 with pl. XXVIII.
149 *Sic* also A. Dodson,'Psusennes II and Shoshenq', 1993, p. 268. Jansen-Winkeln, *Inschriften der Spätzeit* I, 2007, p.220 mentions that the inscription is no proof of the tomb decoration being contemporary.

ḥ3wty, 'chief commander'.[150] One might argue that this latter inscription belonged to the person depicted with a full head of hair, and that the priestly title pertained to another figure behind him. However, the sketch of the scene in Hay MSS 29824,2 verso and the accompanying description appear to indicate that this was the end of the register.

It is a regrettable fact that we know virtually nothing of the high ranking priests of Amun at Thebes in the reign of Psusennes II. As for the time of Sheshonk I, it is known that he appointed his son Iuput as high priest of Amun (and army leader) but there is no evidence of the king's authority having been accepted at Thebes prior to his year 5.[151] An attempt at an identification has been suggested by D. Aston.[152] This is based on the appearance of an ushabti-figure (see below) attributed to our tomb-owner. Aston would prefer to identify the high priest referred to in Amenemopet's tomb as Menkheperra A, Smendes II or Pinedjem II. Hence he would date the tomb to ca. 1000-950 B.C.

The inscription in the funerary scene (fig. 53) is even more intriguing. The recitations performed salute ('the great big praised one') and ('the great majesty') and then go on to acclaim Amun and 'the one who made for him a life-time of truth'; they refer to someone who 'completed 88 years seeing Amun', and who 'follows Amun' and 'follows the royal ka of his lord'. The precise information presented here seems to be that Amenemopet saw himself as being in the service of the god, but perhaps only until the moment his sovereign passed away. The word and should be taken as complimentary designations for our tomb-owner, though combined with the writing for it may appear to confuse the issue as to whose funeral we are witnessing. The 88 years consequently refer to the age of Amenemopet himself. Since he mentions following the royal ka of his lord, rather than following in the footsteps of his lord (as an 18th-dynasty court official would have described his career), it would seem that Amenemopet's sovereign may have departed this life at the time the inscription was composed. At the age of 88 Amenemopet would probably have retired from active service, but he could still be making reference to the king in whose reign he had performed his duties in the temple of Amun, in spite of the fact that a new king would have succeeded him on the throne. If he died in the reign of Sheshonk I, he would have been a minimum of 67 years old when this king came to the throne.

A possible interpretation of the nature of the inscription could be that it was a biographical text recording a visit by Amenemopet to the north, perhaps on the occasion of the instalment of a new king, where Amenemopet presented himself at court and was praised by the sovereign, a fact which he reported on his return to Thebes and eventually commemorated in the decoration of his tomb.

Although a substantial number of Thebans of the 21st and 22nd dynasties are known from the burials in the two caches at Deir el-Bahari, few decorated tombs of the period have come to light. Out of the five extant tombs (TT nos. 68, 70, 307, 337 and 348) four are known to have been usurped.[153] The owner took over an existing tomb and appropriated it by changing the name, but apparently without altering the decoration of the monument. The owner of TT 307, however, seems also to have been responsible for the wall-decoration of his tomb,[154] but it was left unfinished, and the shape of the room is that of the hall of a typical 18th-dynasty tomb.

150 J. Capart, 'Quelques figurines funeraires d'Amenemopet', 1940, p. 191 takes this person to be Herihor. *Sic* also S. Binder, *The Gold of Honour*, 2008, pp. 142-143.

151 K. Kitchen, *Third Intermediate Period*, 1973, pp. 288-9.

152 Personal communication 1989.

153 In his article 'Die thebanische Nekropole der 21. Dynastie', 2002, pp. 348ff. T. Kikuchi discusses TT 68, 291, 320 and MMA 60 in connection with usurped tombs, but chiefly with regard to architectural layout. Little was recorded of this for TT A18. Jansen-Winkeln includes copies of some inscriptions from TT 68 (p. 220) and also refers to TT 70 (p. 221).

We should therefore consider whether our Amenemopet used a similar method of acquiring a funerary monument for himself and his family at a time when the tradition of decorating private monuments appears to have approached a stand-still. As already mentioned, the subjects chosen for the walls of Amenemopet's tomb do not differ substantially from those found in a Ramessid tomb, but the inscriptions point to a later date. If they are not contemporary with the scenes to which they pertain, they would have been completely rewritten. Although in the case of the name of Pa[n]maet this appears to have been squeezed in later, the only place which gives cause for concern is the inscription behind the military person in the 'rewarding scene'. The inscriptions elsewhere are very compact, but here space was left blank which could perhaps have been used. Only a study of the original painting would reveal if it actually was, and whether it was erased or altered.

The decoration of the tomb

According to Rosellini (MSS 284 G63 verso) the decoration was painted with very fine contours. His publication in colour of the scene with the funerary rites shows that the background here was white. 'Space' inside hieroglyphs was indicated in yellow. Hay reports that 'the subjects are much destroyed but what remains of them is interesting' (MSS 29824,1 verso).
The entry in the Hay MSS concerns 'the chamber', i.e. just one room. The decoration he describes is on 'the right side' and on the 'left side'. There is no specific mention of front and rear walls, but it would seem nevertheless that some of the scenes were positioned on a rear wall of a chamber, on either side of a door leading further into the tomb. We must also keep in mind what Hay said about the state of the tomb when he saw it. The subjects which were sketched by Hay, and copied in greater detail by Champollion and Rosellini, appear to have been in excellent condition. If the destruction of the scenes had been carried out intentionally for the purpose, for example, of removing portions of painted plaster, it is more than likely that this would have occurred in the registers containing 'offering scenes' or 'relatives' - an ever popular target for tomb robbers.

Doorway

Somewhere 'at the doorway' Wilkinson copied an inscription which was mentioned above (MSS v.150 and 151). This was published in his *Materia Hieroglyphica*, Malta 1828, pl. v. To the left, the text was inked in and the signs appear to be in their original position (with a correction at the end of the middle column), whereas in the pencilled copy on the following page, the column on the right has been broken up into two.

… ḥr pꜥ[sbꜣ ḫꜣ] m niwt- mriimn sḫnt.f r wḥm ḥsw.f in nb tꜣwy nsw bit ḥḏḫprrꜥ[155] …

154 *Sic* also D. Aston's review of A. Niwinski, '21st Dynasty Coffins from Thebes' in *JARCE* 28, 1992, p. 233.

Fig. 50 Wilkinson MSS v.150 and 151 (from *JEA* 79, 1993, pl. XXVIII).

'... Psusennes beloved-of-Amun, his being promoted to ...repeating his praise by the Lord of the Two Lands, King of Upper and Lower Egypt Hedjkheperra...'

Dodson[156] reads the initial letter in Wilkinson's copy as , and restores a and a in the hatched areas to complete the cartouche of Psusennes and suggests the addition of the first cartouche of Psusennes in this column. In the 2nd column he restores the last word as *mꜣʿ* 'present, offer' or 'lead, guide, direct; send, despatch'. In the 3rd column he reads for and inserts the second cartouche of Sheshonq. In the existing cartouche he restores *stp n rʿ*. The sun disk can be made out, but Wilkinson's sketches both show an inexplicable vertical sign to the left.

As copied by Wilkinson, signs are missing on the page where he inserted 'at the doorway'. In the middle column there would be room for preceding the cartouche.

The doorway in question is probably the entrance doorway, although in theory it could be another one, leading to a second chamber. The text is written in hieroglyphs, not in hieratic, in vertical columns as if pertaining to a proper scene or being an autobiographical inscription which continued further down on the wall (Dodson: 'it is difficult to ascertain how much is lost'). The initial part of the text, preceding our '1st column' is also lost. If there were an illustration to go with this inscription, it would show its author facing left. It is possible, though, that hieroglyphs filled in the entire inner jamb of the entrance door. It is interesting that we have an unusual detail of biography on the right wall of the chamber (the funeral procession), and that the tomb-owner is depicted being rewarded. Rather than being a graffito, the text at the doorway is thus more likely to be an integral part of the tomb decoration.

155 Reading *ḫpr* for *ḥḏ*, see above p. 72.
156 'Psusennes II and Shoshenq I' 1993, p. 268 with discussion of the evidence from TT A18.

Right wall

Upper register: Scene A Rewarding scene
Scene B Funeral procession
Lower register: Scene C Offerings to the tomb-owner

Scene A
Rewarding scene

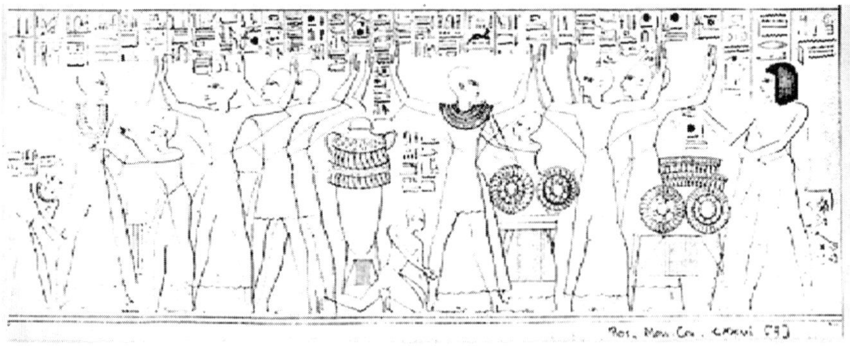

Fig. 51 Rosellini, *Mon. civ.* cxxvi [7]

Hay MSS 29816,137 (detail of deceased) with description and sketch of entire scene in 29824,1 verso - 2 verso; Rosellini, *Mon. civ.* cxxvi [7]; Binder, *Gold of Honour*, pp.142-144.

This subject must have been positioned on the upper part of a wall, as opposed to a scene mentioned in the following by Hay which is said to be 'in the lower line'. It was sketched by Hay (MSS 29824,2 verso, middle) with two details with the tomb-owner drawn in Hay MSS 29816,137. It was recorded in its entirety by Rosellini (*Mon. civ.* cxxxvi [7]) (not, it would seem, 'incomplete' as stated in the *Top. Bibl.* p. 453). The Hay sketch of scenes A and B are in two registers in his small notebook, divided by a single line. Above, separated from the rest by a double line, are subjects which would appear to belong on the left wall (see below). Scenes A and B may have formed one continuous register.

Fig. 52 Hay MSS 29824,2 verso

The subject depicted is inspired by a well-known motif seen since the Amarna Period and sporadically in Ramessid tombs.[157] Here, however, the necklaces given to the tomb-owner appear to be floral, not golden and we do not see a king distributing them, but a military person lends an official air to the scene. The description by Hay of this scene, accompanied by his very summary sketch, corresponds to the more detailed drawing in Rosellini's publication.

157 See S. Binder, *Gold of Honour*, 2008.

The ceremony takes place in the presence of a person at the extreme[158] right:

→

hrw pn n iri ḫrw ꜥꜣt n imn r-ꜥ[159] *it nṯr ḥm (nṯr) tpi n imn (…?) imy-r mšꜥ wr ḥꜣwty*

'The day of making the great roar to Amun next to the god's father (and) high-priest of Amun (…?) generalissimo, chief commander' (for the identity of this person, see also above, p. 73).

In front of the military man, also facing left, are four of the tomb-owner's relatives. From left to right they are identified as 1) *sꜣ.f ḏdmntiwfꜥnḫ* 'his son, Djementef'ankh, justified', 2) *hy n sꜣt.f ḫnswms mꜥꜣ ḫrw,* 'husband of his daughter, Khensmosi'; 3) *pdḫns mꜥꜣ ḫrw* 'Pedekhons, justifie"; and 4) *ꜥnḫfnḫnsw mꜥꜣ ḫrw* 'Ankhefenkhons, justified'. These four persons, facing the tomb-owner, raise their arms in acclamation.

A relative of the tomb-owner adjusts his collar. He is *hy n sꜣt.f ḥm nṯr imn nsimn mꜣꜥ ḫrw* 'husband of his daughter, prophet of Amun, Nesamun, justified.' Another embraces his leg: *sꜣ n sꜣ.f it nṯr n imn šs mḏꜣt imnmipt* 'his grandson, god's father of Amun, document scribe[160] Amenemopet, justified'. The tomb-owner himself, facing right with raised arms, is identified as *ḥm nṯr imn-rꜥ nsw nṯrw ḥri sštꜣ ḥri sš mḏꜣt*[160] *n pr imn imnmipt mꜣꜥ ḫrw* 'prophet of Amun-Ra, king of the gods, chief of secrets, head of document scribes of the estate of Amun, Amenemopet, justified.' The figures are separated in three groups by necklaces on stands and from the following scene by a tall vase decorated with floral garlands. The collar around Amenopet's neck is a floral collar, not the golden collar seen in other rewarding scenes. In Hay MSS 29816,137 part of the necklace was drawn in colour (yellow, blue, red and white).

A similar scene follows on the left. Relatives of the tomb-owner facing left being once more (from right to left):

1) *hy n sꜣt.f pt n pr imn ꜥnḫfḫnsw mꜣꜥ' ḫrw sꜣ n it ntr mry (ntr) hri pt*[162] *nḫtimn mꜣꜥ ḫrw*
'husband of his daughter, (head of the) kitchen in the estate of Amun Ankhefkhons, son of the god's father beloved of the (god), head of the kitchen(?) Nakhtamun, justified'.

2) *hy n sꜣt.f it nṯr mry (nṯr) ḥri n šd*[163] *pdḫnsw mꜣꜥ ḫrw*
'husband of his daughter, god's father beloved (of the god), head of readers Pedekhons, justified'.

3) *hy n sꜣt.f it ntr mry (ntr) hri n šd n pr imn ḫnswms* 'husband of his daughter, gods father beloved (of the god), head of readers of the estate of Amun, Khensmosi, justified'.

4) *sꜣ.f [it] ntr mry (ntr) ḏdmntiwfꜥnḫ mꜣꜥ ḫrw* 'His son, god's [father] beloved of (the god) Djementef'ankh, justified'.

The tomb-owner stands with his arms raised as before with a near identical legend to the previous one: *ḥm nṯr n imnrꜥ nsw nṯrw ḥry sštꜣ ḥry sš mḏꜣw*[164] *n pr imn imnmipt mꜣꜥ ḫrw sꜣ ꜥnḫy mꜣꜥ ḫrw* 'prophet of Amun-Ra, king of the gods, chief of secrets chief of document scribes of the estate of Amun, Amenemipet, son of Ankhy, justified.'[165] He is once more assisted by

158 The scene appears to conclude here.

159 K. Jansen-Winkeln, *Inschriften der Spätzeit I*, 2007, p. 218 reads *rpꜥ*.

160 K. Jansen-Winkeln, *Inschriften der Spätzeit I*, 2007, p. 218 reads *sš ḳdwt*, adding *(sic)*.

161 K. Jansen-Winkeln, *Inschriften der Spätzeit I*, 2007, p. 218 reads *sš ḳdwt*, adding *(sic)*.

162 For an identical writing cf. TT B3 below. The usual word for kitchen at this time would be *wꜥbt*. Jansen-Winkeln reads *p (sic)t*. In both instances the word appears to be garbled.

163 Written or copied as .

164 Jansen-Winkeln reads *sš ḳd.*

165 Binder, *Gold of Honour*, 2008, p. 144 suggest the possibility of seeing in this person Piankh, Herihor's father-in-law.

 *hy n sꜣt.f hm nṯr n imn sš nṯr ḥwt n pr imn nsimn* 'husband of his daughter, prophet of Amun, scribe in the temple of [Amun] in the estate of Amun, Nesamun.'
His leg is embraced by 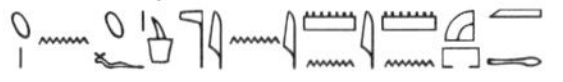 *sꜣ n sꜣ.f it nṯr in imn imn-mipt mꜣꜥ ḫrw* 'his grandson, god's father of Amun, Amenemopet, justified'.

The generalissimo has his own black hair, whereas everybody else is clean shaven as befits their genuinely priestly status. But in both cases Nesamun wears a pointed cap.
The register thus presents us with more or less duplicate scenes with identical actors, but with the military man omitted in one of them. It is the day of the 'big roar'.

Scene B
Funeral procession

Fig. 53 Rosellini, *Mon. civ.* cxxvii (upper)

Hay MSS 29824,2-2 verso (description and sketch); Rosellini, *Mon. civ.* cxxvii; sarcophagus and oxen: Lüddekens in *MDAIK* xi, 1943, pp. 158-60, fig. 55 (from Rosellini); mummy and attendants: Wilkinson MSS v.170 [middle].

This scene was apparently situated to the left of the rewarding scene, for Hay describes the above from right to left.[166] The scene was rendered in sketch by Hay, below the rewarding scene (cf. fig. 52), but the pages of his notebook are very small, and, as mentioned above, we should not take it for granted that this was the arrangement of the scenes on the wall itself.
The episodes chosen are the dragging of the shrine by a pair of oxen and purifying the mummy. The former shows an upright rectangular shrine on a boat, placed on a sledge and pulled by the oxen, assisted by two men and a third with a stick in his hand. An Anubis on a shrine in front of the box may be a reference to the tomb-owner's title 'head of secrets', sometimes

166 Jansen-Winkeln prefers to place the funeral procession below the rewarding scene.

written in this fashion. Adjoining this scene to the left is one of the rituals taking place in front of the mummy, elsewhere shown as standing up in front of the tomb. The mummy is being held in a near vertical position by *s3.f ḏdmntiw.fˁnḫ m3ˁ ḫrw* 'his son, Djedmentefankh, justified,' while a person by the name of Pa[n]maˁet[167] pours red myrrh over it. The 'widow' sits at the mummy's feet with her hand to her face and her hair dishevelled. Two loaves are placed near by. The act is described as *ir(t) m3ˁ ḫrw*[168] *n tf ḥm nṯr n imn-rˁ nsw nṯrw imnmipt m3ˁ ḫrw* 'Performing justification for his father, prophet of Amun-Ra, king of the gods, Amenemopet, justified'. In an unusual oblique inscription the kneeling widow is also described as taking part in the ritual of *irt m3ˁ ḫrw* 'performing justification'.[169]

The text continues from left to right as follows:

ḏd mdw ih3 sp sn n p3 ḥs wr ˁ3 ih3 [n] p3 ḥm wr ḥsn.sn imn ih3 n[.f] irn.f ˁḥˁw n m3ˁ't nb iw km.f rnpt 88 ḥr m3 imn r r-ˁ ḥtp.f iw šms.f imn wḏ3 iw šms.f k3 nsw n nb.f wḏ3 ihn n gr hn iḫ3 nfrti.f wsir ḥm nṯr n imn imnmipt m3ˁ ḫrw

'Words to be recited: Hail! Hail to the great big praised one! Hail to the great majesty! They have praised Amun.[170] Hail to [him]! He has spent a life-time of all truth, completing 88 years seeing Amun until he set, following Amun healthy, following the royal ka of his lord healthy. O rejoice without ceasing! Rejoice! Remember his perfection, Osiris, prophet of Amun, Amenemopet, justified'.

The frequent references to Amun must be seen partly in the light of the occupation of the tomb-owner, partly in relation to the contemporary efforts to promote this god. The entire family of Amenemopet was closely involved with the administration of the estate of Amun. It is interesting that we have the biographical detail about Amenemopet's age included in what would usually be a conventional funerary text.

Scene C
Offering to king Amenhotpe I and queen Ahhotep

Champollion, *Mon.* cliii (3); Rosellini, *Mon. stor.* xxix,1 [left]; parts of text id. *Text* iii, pl. i,21; Hay MSS 29824,1 verso and 2 (description); Rosellini MSS 284, G 63 verso; Wilkinson MSS v.150.

Hay describes this as follows: 'another subject is the Gentleman and Lady seated as God and Goddess, the former has a stick in his hand, with an offering table before him, the names I have copied belong to them.' The royal persons and texts were drawn and published by Rosellini, but Champollion is the only one who includes the representation of the tomb-owner as being part of the scene.
The deified king and queen (his maternal grandmother) are seated to the left, facing right, their accompanying inscriptions being as follows:[171]

167 In Rosellini's copy these signs are almost part of the tomb-owner's name, but written immediately above the person's head.
168 Written/copied as .
169 As above erroneously copied by Rosellini. Wilkinson also copied for . This was maintained by Jansen-Winkeln, *Inschriften der Spätzeit I*, 2007, p. 219.
170 See also E. Lüddekens, 'Totenklagen', 1943, pp. 158-60.
171 For the epithets of the king see below, pp.82-83.

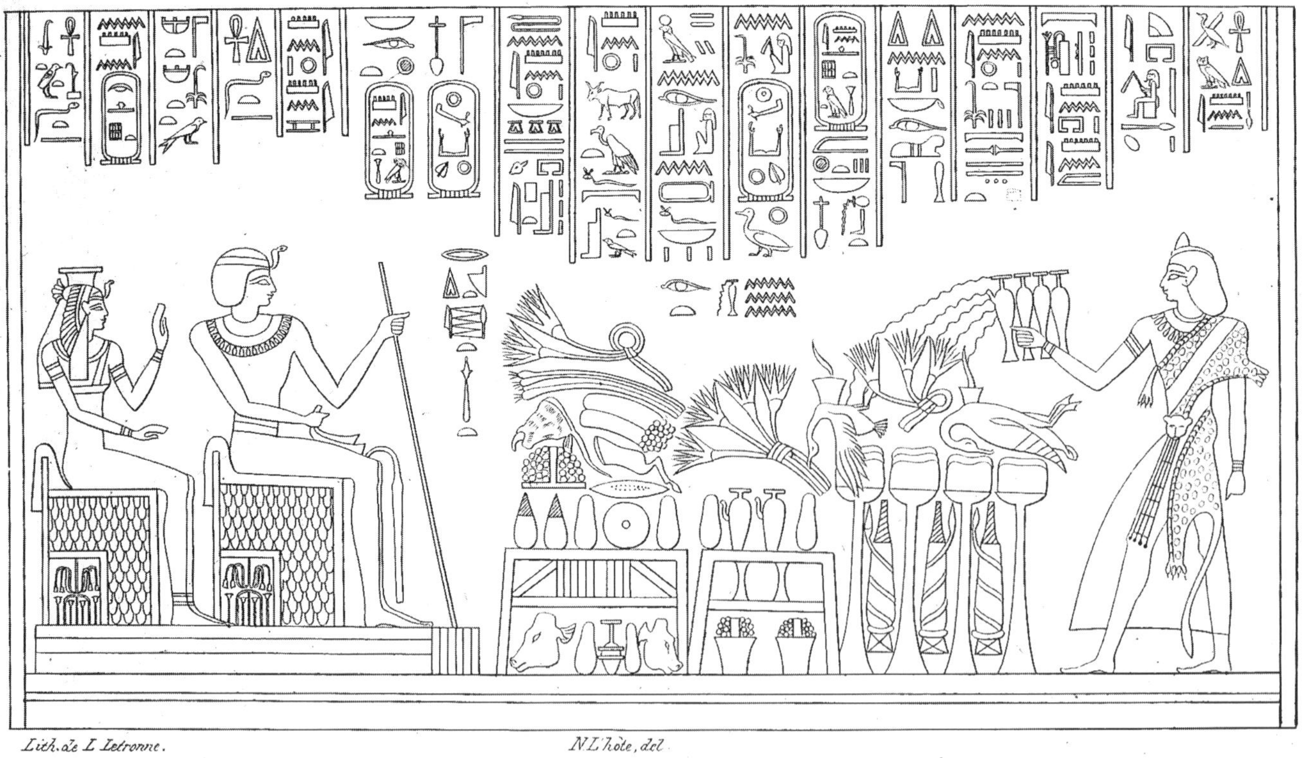

Fig. 54 Champollion, *Mon.* cliii (3)

nṯr nfr ḏsrkꜣrꜥ ỉwꜥ rꜥ nb ỉr ḫt ỉmnḥtp (n t)ꜣ bnrt sꜣ ỉmn mry ỉmn dỉ ꜥnḫ ḏt ḥmt nṯr ḥmt nsw wrt n ỉmn ỉꜥḥḥtp ꜥnḫti rnpti ḏt

'Good god, Djeserkara heir-of-Ra, Amenhotpe (of) the date palm,[172] son of Amun, beloved of Amun, given life for ever. God's wife, king's great wife of Amun, Ahhotep, given life and youth for ever'.

The text accompanying the actual offering was recorded as follows:

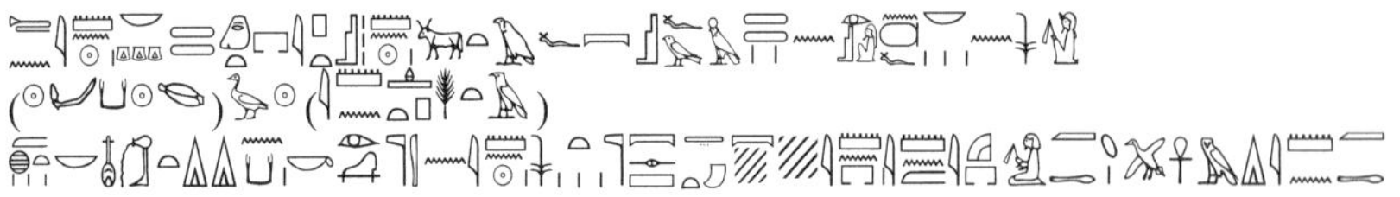

wdn n ỉmn-rꜥ nb nswt tꜣwy ḫnty ipt-st ỉmn-rꜥ kꜣmwtf ḥri st.f wr ḥr-ꜣḫti n wsir n rn.f nbw n nsw ḏsrkꜣrꜥ ỉwꜥ rꜥ sꜣ rꜥ ỉmḥhtp (n) tꜣ bnrt m ḫt nb nfrt wꜥbt dd n kꜣ.k wsir ḥm nṯr n ỉmn-rꜣ nsw nṯrw ḥri sštꜣ ḥri... pr ỉmn ỉmnmipt mꜣꜥ' ḫrw sꜣ pꜣꜥnhmdiỉmn mꜣꜥ ḫrw

'Offering to Amun-Ra, lord of the thrones of the Two Lands, foremost in Karnak, Amun-Ra bull-of-his-mother, chief of his great throne, (to) Harakhti, to Osiris in all his names, to King Djeserkara heir-of-Ra, Amenhotpe (of the date palm) (an offering consisting of) all good and pure things, perpetually given to your ka, Osiris, prophet of Amun-Ra, king of the gods, head of secrets, head [of letterwriters of the] estate of Amun, Amenemopet, justified, son of Paꜥankhemdiamun, justified'.

172 A. von Lieven, 'Kleine Beiträge', 2001, pp. 43 and 54-6. K. Jansen-Winkeln, *Inschriften der Spätzeit I*, 2007, p. 219 sees a papyrus instead of a palm tree.

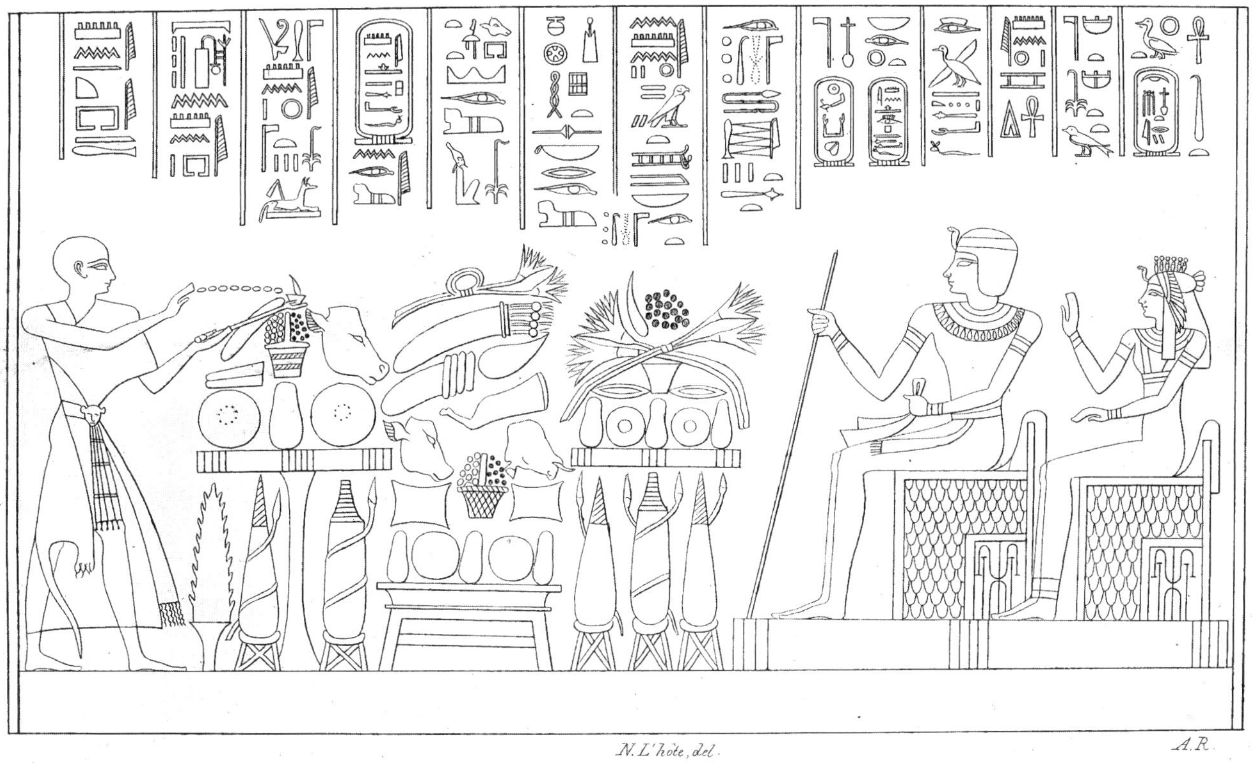

Fig. 55 Champollion, *Mon.* cliii (4)

Above the offering is written
rdit ꜥ3bt ꜥ3t 'making a great offering'
and
irt kbḥt 'making cool water'.

Scene D
Offerings to the deceased

Having described these funerary scenes in MSS 29824,2 Hay goes on to say: 'The lower line is also(?) different offerings before the Gentleman with the exception of a subject drawn from the opposite side of the wall.' This latter subject must be our scene C. This leaves 'different offerings' to fill in the remaining part of the lower register of the right wall. None of these were copied.

Scene E
Offering to king Amenhotpe I and queen Ahmose Nefertere

Champollion, *Mon.* cliii (4); Rosellini, *Mon. stor.* xxix right; head of queen ibid. i,2; part of text, *Text*, iii, pl. i,22; Hay MSS 29824, 2 verso [upper left]; Rosellini MSS 284, G64; Wilkinson MSS v.150; Lepsius MSS 429.

The two deities are seated in an identical fashion to that described above, but facing left. In the publication of Rosellini, the headdress of the queen is depicted in the greatest detail, and he included a separate drawing of the queen's face and name. The inscription above identifies them as

ntr nfr ḏsrk3rʿ iwʿ nb ir ḫt imnḥtp rs p t3 ʿ3.f ptr p3 t3 ʿ3.f mry Imn-Rʿ di ʿnḫ
ḥmt nṯr ḥmt nsw wrt s3t rʿ iʿḥms-nfrtiry ʿnḫti

'Good god, Djeserkara, heir (of Ra), lord of rituals, Amenhotpe whose greatness the country beholds, whose greatness the country beholds,[173] beloved of Amun-Ra, given life.
God's wife, great royal wife, daughter of Ra, Ahmosi Nefertere, may she live!'

The queen is depicted in her black manifestation, designating her as mother not only of Amenhotpe I, but of the entire 18th dynasty.[174] In contrast, the complexion of queen Ahhotep was described as 'white' by Wilkinson, while Hay called it 'yellow'.

The text above the tomb-owner says

irt sntr wdn ʿ3bt ʿ3t n imn-rʿ ḥr3ḫti tm nb iwnw ptḥ-skr-wsir ḫnty imntt wsir nsw imnḥtp ptr p3 t3 ʿ3.f in wsir ḥm nṯr n imn-rʿ nsw nṯrw ḥri sšty3 ḥri sš mḏ3wt n pr imn imnmipt m3ʿ ḫrw

'Presenting incense (and) making a great offering to Amun-Ra, Harakhti, Atum, lord of Heliopolis, Ptah-Sokar-Osiris, who is foremost of the West, Osiris king Amenhotpe who-watches-over-the-land by Osiris, prophet of Amun-Ra, king of the gods, head of secrets, head of letter writers of the estate of Amun, Amenemopet, justified'.

Above the offerings is written

 *irt sntr* 'making incense'

The offerings consist of lotus flowers, grapes, cucumber or melon, loaves of bread, jars of wine or beer, and two fruits split open. They are being consecrated by a priest with a censer as also sketched by Hay:

Fig. 56 Hay MSS 29824,2 verso [upper left]

In both scenes, more deities are mentioned in the text than were represented.

A study of the cult of Amenhotpe I has recently been made by A. von Lieven[175] who gives numerous examples for the period after the end of the New Kingdom. Failing contemporary tombs and temples, coffins of the 21st dynasty, shabti boxes and linen have proven to be a good source. The epithets of the

173 The epithet inside the cartouche has been repeated.
174 See L. Manniche, 'The complexion of queen Ahmosi Nefertere', 1979, pp. 11-19.
175 'Kleine Beiträge zur Vergöttlichung Amenophis I', 2000, pp. 103-21 and 2001, pp. 41-64.

king, including those written inside his cartouches, are consistent with finds of this date: 'heir of Ra (designating a solar manifestation of the king)' 'of the date palm',[176] 'whose greatness etc.'[177] At this time, the cult of the deified king is closely related to that of Amun and Osiris, which at least explains why these two are included in the offering text in our tomb. These epithets are clear proof of the date of the inscriptions.

Scene F Man with tablet
Scene G Deity with child
Scene H Guests
Scene I Weighing scene

We have to rely entirely on Hay for these subjects. 'On the left side is a seated man with pen and ink stand in his hand, employed in writing hieroglyphs on a tablet supported by a youth on both hands. - a man or woman(?) follows with a child on the knee offering a bunch of grapes with one hand while the other is on the shoulder of the child taking another bunch from the hand of an attendant. - Guests male and female are seated in lines in the usual manner (MSS 29824, 1 verso-2 verso)'.

Scene F
Man with 'tablet'

Hay MSS 29816,136 with description in 298124, 2; re-drawn by M. Baud for *Les dessins ébauchés de la nécropole thébaine,* Paris 1935, and also by the present writer in *City of the Dead*, fig. 65.

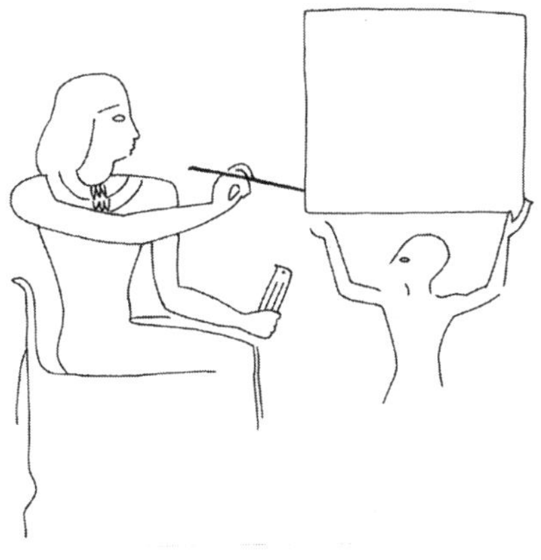

Fig. 57 Hay 29816,136 (re-drawn by LM)

This must be a unique representation of Amenemopet shown while performing his duties as a document scribe in the estate of Amun, and it may be taken as an indication that writing, not drawing was among his duties. The drawing reproduced by Baud, as well as the one previously presented by the present writer, gives no clue to the nature of the document that Amenemopet was preparing. But a closer look at the original Hay MSS reveals that there were traces of hieroglyphs on the page. The rows of signs, written out above by Hay, reproduce the characters he was able to distinguish:

Fig. 58 Hay MSS 29816,136 (re-drawn by LM)

It is slightly puzzling that the letter was written in hieroglyphic script as opposed to hieratic.

176 See especially pp. 54ff for this epithet used in the 21st - 22nd dynasty.
177 TT A18, dated to the 21st dynasty, is mentioned on p. 43 of von Lieven's 'Kleine Beiträge', 2001.

Scene G
Deity with child

Hay MSS 29824,2 verso [upper right] and description 29824,2.

Fig. 59 Hay MSS 29824,2 verso [upper right] (re-drawn by LM)

This was by the *Top. Bibl.* interpreted as 'Termuthis suckling child'. The group sketched by Hay shows the deity(?) seated on a throne, facing right with an infant across her lap and a servant(?) standing on her right. Termuthis, or Renenwetet, is usually represented as a serpent; the accompanying child can be either Nepri, the corn god, as for example in TT 57, or the king, as in TT 48. But in her role as mother, goddess of destiny and funerary goddess, the anthropoid or mixed form was obviously preferred.[178] In our case we have the anthropoid goddess, but she is not the 'Renenwetet lactans' kown from other sources, for the goddess feeds grapes(?), not milk to the infant, a detail which was also depicted in an earlier 'lost' tomb in the area, TT A11.[179] There may be a connection between the presence of this goddess and the profession of the owner of our tomb.[180]

Scene H
Guests

Hay MSS 29824, 2 (brief mention).

'Guests male+female are seated in lines in the usual manner'.

On the opposite ('right') wall offerings before the tomb-owner were positioned in a lower register, and this was probably the arrangement on this wall as well. Whether the persons depicted were 'guests' is another matter, as traditional banquet scenes were not common in post 18th-dynasty tombs. However, named individuals appear in a similar context in some Ramessid tombs.

Scene I
Weighing scene

When describing the left wall of the tomb (MSS 29824,2-2 verso) and the row of guests 'seated in lines in the usual manner' Hay adds a dash - and continues: 'the remains of a weighing subject is left, with Typhon sitting on top of the balance. A feather is in the scales that remains perfect – the scales are I think always made well poised.' In a new paragraph follows mention of Amenhotpe I and the black Ahmosi Nefertere. It would seem that the weighing scene belonged somewhere on the left wall (*sic* also tentatively *Top. Bibl.*), and, in that the entry about the royal couple is in a separate paragraph, the weighing scene would be in an upper register, which is exactly where one would expect to find it.

Our scene was mentioned by C. Seeber[181] as being positioned on the left wall. The choice of figures seated on top of the scales stands between the common baboon (Thoth) and, more rarely, an ibis, a falcon, Anubis or a man.

178 See J. Brockhuis, *De godin Renenwetet*, 1971, pp. 50-4; *LdÄ* V, col. 234, fn 11-12.

179 See L. Manniche, *Lost Tombs,* 1988, p. 51, ill. 8 (left).

180 See G. Fecht, 'Schicksalgöttinnen', 1978, p. 25; also p. 27 and p. 32 n. 50 relating a person's lifespan to a divine plan (cf. above p. 73 'the one who made for him a life-time of truth').

181 *Untersuchungen zur Darstellung des Totengerichts im Alten Ägypten,* 1976, p. 68.

Position of the scenes

In his notes on this tomb, Rosellini confirms that the scenes with the royal couples were positioned to the right and left in the tomb, but he adds that they were on either side of a 'second doorway' ('a destra della 2a porta seggono il re (Amenophis I)… e la regina (Ahhotep)'. Here we have an indication that the tomb consisted of more than just the one room. The two subjects C and E would undoubtedly have formed a symmetrical representation, even if not represented on the same (rear) wall. For his publication Rosellini (who omits the tomb-owner) arranged the two groups so as to face each other in one and the same scene. This would be an atypical lay-out.[182]

We can now begin to have a clearer impression of the distribution of the scenes on the right and left with the proviso that some of them may have extended to the rear and even the front wall. In the right part we have in the upper register the funeral, moving towards the west, directly followed (towards the entrance) by the rewarding scene. Below, the tomb-owner adoring Amenhotpe I and queen Ahhotep and behind him offering to the tomb-owner. On the left in the lower register the tomb-owner offering to Amenhotpe I and his mother and, behind the tomb-owner, a row of relatives and/or guests. In the register above the weighing scene, presumably at the innermost part of the wall, followed by the deity with child and man with tablet. The position of the latter two is highly conjectural, as they are both atypical scenes.

It remains to be considered whether the inscription copied by Wilkinson 'at the doorway' could possibly be directly related to any of the motifs described so far. As the upper right register is already complete, the only other option would be to place it near the 'man with tablet' who can hardly be anyone but the tomb-owner. As the inscription faces in the wrong direction, this can be ruled out. It must therefore belong either on jamb of the doorway itself or on one of the front walls next to the doorway, presumably being part of an autobiographical inscription.

Finds in the tomb?

Shabti box

In Hay MSS 29824,1 verso [upper left] we find a pair of cartouches of Amenhotpe I with the following comment: 'names on a box found by P(iccinini) in a tomb behind the Mummy Tomb'. As our tomb was also behind the 'mummy tomb', and because of the additional *iaw* inside the king's cartouche, there is a certain likelihood that the box originally belonged in TT A18.

According D. Aston[183] the box, which no doubt contained shabtis, was probably a 'large' box, in which case it must date from before 900 BC. The cartouches suggest that it is of the 'pictorial' type, rather than the 'inscriptional' type. Such pictorial boxes, with three lids, also died out around 900 BC, having been introduced in the 20th dynasty. Two-lidded boxes of similar design began somewhat later around 1100-1050 BC.

The cartouches are drawn as seen on fig. 60.

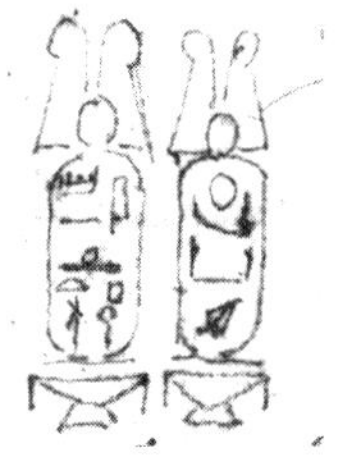

Fig. 60 Hay MSS 29824,1 verso

182 K. Jansen-Winkeln, *Inschriften der Spätzeit I*, 2007, p. 219 places scene C on the left and scene E on the right of the rear wall ('hintere Wand').

183 Personal communication 1989, cf. D. Aston, 'The Shabti Box', 1994, pp. 27-8, where our box is, however, not mentioned.

One may compare this box with another box with the cartouche of Amenophis I in the collections of The Brooklyn Museum, no.37.1524E.[184] It is of a type with three compartments generally believed to have ceased to be in use around year 980 B.C., that is to say during or before the last decade of the 21st dynasty.[185] The god's father Ankhefkhons son of the god's father Ankhef(Amon?) named on the box is undoubtedly a different individual from the counter of grain Ankhefkhons, son-in-law of our tomb-owner. Another box, possibly from the same burial, is in Berlin inv. 251 = *LD* III, 4d. A third box in Berlin *LD* III, 4c belonged to this man's daughter.

The exact shape and size of the box seen by Hay is not known, and apart from the possible 21st dynasty context of its discovery, we are left with the orthography of the royal names which is rather different. Hay's copy writes the two names in two cartouches, whereas the Brooklyn box has the two names together in one cartouche (twice). Hay's copy includes the epithets 'heir of (Ra)' and 'ruler of Thebes' respectively, whereas the Brooklyn box may have 'ruler of Thebes' in the second cartouche (the signs are indistinct).[186]

Shabtis

If Piccinini found a shabti box in the tomb of Amenemope, its contents would no doubt have been intact. Shabtis of a man of this name have indeed appeared on the market. Three are now in Brussels.[187] A fourth is in a private collection in Belgium.[188] The text was included in Jansen-Winkeln's publication (p. 220). The owner's title here appears as sS qdwt.

Book of the Dead

An unpublished papyrus in Cairo (JE 95713) very likely belonged to our tomb-owner.[189] Here his father's name is given as Ankhy, which may be an abbreviation for Paankhemduamu, known from the tomb.

184 Letter from R. Fazzini 11th August 1989.

185 D. Aston, personal communiucation 1989, cf. Aston, 'The Shabti box', 1994, type V.

186 Note on cards in The Brooklyn Museum.

187 J. Capart, 'Quelques figurines funéraires d'Amenemopet', 1940, pp. 190ff. Capart reads *sš kdwt* for *sš mḏ3t.*

188 Personal communication.

189 K. Jansen-Winkeln, *Inschriften der Spätzeit I,* 2007, p. 220 and A. Niwinski, *Funerary Papyri*, 1989, 262.

B3

The tomb was at the Khokha hill, north of TT 200 (*sic Top. Bibl.*).[190] It was visited by James Burton who had joined Hay and Wilkinson at Thebes in 1824. He made neat, pencilled sketches of two scenes, and later Lepsius copied a few texts, but says that he was unable to locate the owner's name. Nevertheless a name appears in one of his copies. He mentions a 'front transverse hall', hence we may deduce that the tomb had more than one room. It was a painted tomb in bad condition ('wenig erhalten'), and the style was 'Reform' and 'setish', an expression elsewhere used by Lepsius to describe 'in the manner of Sethi I'[191] (MSS 292 [lower]). We may interpret this as harking back to the 19th dynasty. The 'paint' would refer to remains of paint on a tomb with decoration in relief as most other late tombs.

The tomb belonged to Hauf, 'head of the kitchen of the estate of Amun'. His father, Nespaiʿohwer, held the same title. Judging from the names, the tomb would appear to date from the Saite period. These two are the only names recorded from the tomb. As the scene in which they belong was not copied, it remains a possibility that the name of Hauf belongs to someone who was not the tomb-owner.

The tomb would be behind the former excavation house of the Metropolitan Museum of Art. A number of earlier tombs are clustered in this area, and one of them, TT 392, appears to be Saite. Most of the known Saite tombs are in the neighbouring area of Assasif. TT 392 has a front transverse hall, followed by a small room. The name of its owner is no longer extant. Future work in this area may reveal a connection.

Scene A
Tomb-owner before deity

The full text of the names as copied by Lepsius, MS 292 [lower left] ran as follows after three destroyed columns of text:

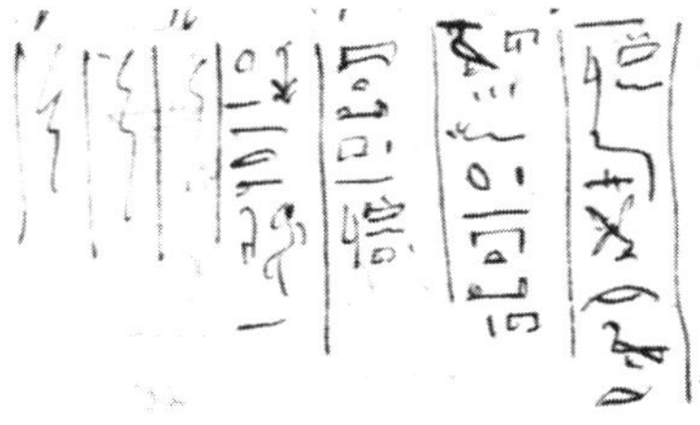

Fig. 61 Lepsius MSS 292 [lower left]

→

… ḫnsw šri(?) ḥri wʿbt[192] *pr imn ḥꜣwf sꜣ n ḥri wʿbt n imn nspꜣiʿḥwr*

'…Khonsu-the-child,[193] chief of the kitchen[194] of the estate of Amun, Hauf, son of the chief of the kitchen of the estate of Amun, Nespaiʿohwer'.

Judging from the direction of the signs, the text would have been written above a representation of the tomb-owner facing left towards a deity. As information is so scarce, every little piece must be considered, and when Lepsius says of the

190 F. Kampp, *Die thebanische Nekropole*, p. 618.
191 I am indebted to J. Osing for deciphering and commenting on this manuscript entry.
192 Identical writing in TT A 18 above, p. 80.
193 The sign after the *r* looks like a lower arm.
194 For *WB* I, 284,3.

text that 'it is placed above him' ('steht über ihm'), we must interpret it to the effect that he (i.e. the tomb-owner, or 'Inhaber' mentioned just above) was depicted immediately below. The inscription was copied in the transverse hall ('in der vordersten Querkammer'). The context as described by Lepsius appears to involve a goddess ('die Göttin' – probably Hathor, as she is referred to in the previous line?) and a 'well ('Brunnen')', but his handwriting is illegible here. Khonsu-the-child may be part of Hauf's titles?

Scene B

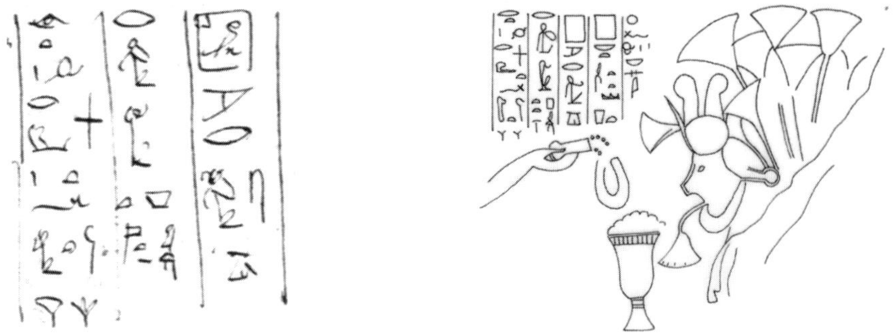

Fig. 62 Lepsius MSS 292 [lower right] and Burton MSS 25644,70 verso [upper]

Offering a menat to the Hathor cow in the mountain

Burton MSS 25644,70 verso [upper]; part of text Lepsius MSS 292 [lower right].

Burton drew the arm of a person and the cow with a bell-shaped (lotiform) 'yellow' vase in between. An accompanying note adds that 'the said cow's leg ought to be on a level with the vase of grass'. The vase thus contained some greenery. The cow is already adorned with a *menat* and is about to receive a second one. The text is as follows (from right to left and thus pertaining to the offering bringer):

←

ḥtḥr mrsgr ḥnwt ỉmntt ỉrt rʿ ỉmỉt r ḥʿt.f hkʿt ?

'Hathor Merseger, Mistress of the West[195], eye of Ra who is at his front, Mistress of the (South and the North?[196])'

and (from left to right)

→

ḥwtḥr nbt ỉmntt ḥnwt ḫf(t) ḥr nb.s ỉ...

'Hathor, Mistress of the West, Mistress who is in front of her Master...'

Although the goddess Mersger was chiefly worshipped at Deir el-Medina in the Ramessid period, a Hathor-Meresger was venerated near Deir el-Bahari.[197] The unfinished TT 177 at Khokha (temp. Ramesses II?) depicts the tomb-owner and his family adoring her on the left rear wall of the hall.[198] One of her epithets was 'eye of Ra'[199] as in this tomb. Another was 'Who is in front of her Master'.[200] In a contemporary coffin an anthropoid form of this latter deity

195 Followed by a *nṯr* sign.

196 In Lepsius' copy, the signs following *ḥkꜣ* appear to depict the flowers of a papyrus (left) and a lotus or lily (right).

197 B. Bruyère, *Mert Seger à Deir el Médineh*, 1929, pp. 193ff.

198 *Top. Bibl.* I, p. 283. An 18th-dynasty stela showing a certain Thonufer before the goddess, is now in the British Museum (56921). A companion to this was found in the temple at Deir el-Bahari (see *Top. Bibl.* II, pp. 395-6).

199 C. Leitz, *Lexikon der ägyptischen Götter und Götterbezeichnungen*, 2002, I, p. 429 d.

200 Leitz, *Lexikon*, III, pp. 343-4.

is depicted behind another female figure offering to the cow in the mountain with a bowl of herbs in between.[201] We should imagine a similar scene on the wall of this tomb showing one deity adoring another, as indicated by the text.

Scene C
Temple pylon

The third scene, sketched by Burton in MSS 25644,70 verso [lower], shows a temple pylon with two flagpoles and a gate. Burton scribbled that the gate was 'dark yellow ochre'. It would be interesting to know which building was referred to here. In view of the occupation of the tomb-owner, it is likely to be a temple of Amun. There was a certain tradition for depicting the temple of Amun in the Theban tombs. If this were the case, it would probably be the second pylon at Karnak.

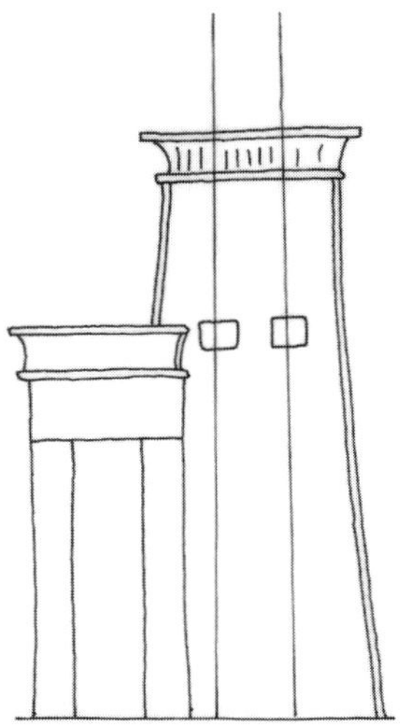

Fig. 63 Burton MSS 25644,70

Position of the scenes

It is tempting to work on the assumption that TT B3 is the same as the much destroyed and unpublished TT 392. Judging from the plan, this would seem to be a disused T-shaped, 18th-dynasty tomb (TT 172 next door is one such). The description by Lepsius of TT B3 suggests a similar shape. TT 392 being located behind the MMA house would fit the general area of el-Biraba and the suggestion by the *Top. Bibl.* of 'north of TT 200'. It is adjacent to TT 203, which he also visited (Lepsius MSS 263). The name of the owner of TT 392 has disappeared. The name of TT B3 was not evident to Lepsius, and it is in any case an unusual one.

Two scenes were recorded in TT 392: funeral in three registers on the right front wall of the hall, and remains of Osiris and a goddess on the left wall of the inner room. A funeral would not normally be found in the hall,[202] but with the change in tomb decoration after the 18th-dynasty this convention was no longer adhered to. Lepsius placed scene A in a transverse hall. It would in theory fit into the right rear wall of the hall in TT 392, the goddess having her back to the inner room, the tomb-owner coming from outside. As the funeral was depicted in the hall, scene B with the Hathor cow emerging from the mountain may also be placed here, preferably on the left rear wall with the mountain closest to the inner room.[203] The pylon is more difficult to assign a place to. Was it perhaps a building connected with the funerary rites? Or it may have been part of a temple.

201 B. Bruyère, *op. cit.*, fig. 103 (no. 6230 belonging to a songstress of Amun).

202 Although there are exceptions, as for example in TT 55 of Ramose.

203 As in TT 177.

TT C14

Very little information is available for this tomb. According to *Top. Bibl.* it was probably located near TT 390-391 at Sheikh ꜥabd el-Qurna.[204] This was confirmed in 2010 in connection with the work of Elena Pischikova engaged in clearing the neighbouring 25th dynasty TT 223 of Karakhamun. TT C14 is to the south of the open court of TT 223, having previously been concealed in the court of one of the village houses. It was blocked with stones and had apparently not been used by the family for a while. The pillared hall of the tomb was only half carved. The north aisle was never finished and the walls and pillars of the south aisle were never decorated. No inscriptions were found here. The cult room was blocked with a wall and not entered. Pischikova suggests a 25th - 26th dynasty date for the tomb, but with reservations as it has not been fully surveyed and excavated. TT 390 is dated to the reign of Psammetichos I, and it was visited by some of the early travellers, including Wilkinson. He appears to be the only one among the early travellers who saw TT C14. In his notebook he mentions it on p. 176 [bottom right], whereas reference to TT 390 is on pp. 169-70. This might suggest that the two tombs were not too distant from each other. TT 391 of the 25th dynasty was mentioned by Wilkinson on the very same page of his MSS as TT C14 in his MSS v.176 [bottom left], and so was TT 390 (MSS v.176 [top and middle].

Judging from the names, TT C14 may be dated to the Saite period. It belonged to  Ankhefendjehuty, called  Neferibra-sonb.

In his comprehensive study of late period tombs at Thebes,[205] D. Eigner also considered TT C14 (pp. 58 and 83), and he attempted to identify it with one of the existing anonymous tombs very close to TT 223 and in the immediate vicinity of TT 390. In his plan of the area (fig. 67), the chamber has been labelled 'TT C14'. In the plan of the chamber itself (fig. 56) it is 'TT C14?' The chamber he suggested, now a store room of the Abdel Rasool family, had no texts left at all which would prove a connection, but it did have a sculpted door (where, according to Eigner, any texts should be sought). It was, however, in the court of TT C14 that Wilkinson copied five vertical lines of text (MSS v.176 [lower right]):

Fig. 64 Wilkinson MSS v.176 [lower right]

mꜣ[…] ḥs.n mwt.f ib.f[…] ꜥwꜣt m rdit ḥr gs […] nb tꜣwy rḫ nḥm m ii sbꜣw imy-r […] ꜥnḫfnḏḥwty rn.f nfr …nfrrꜥsnb

'…seeing… praised by his mother… his heart… robbery by partiality…, Lord of the Two Lands, one who knows how to save(?) the coming of the stars, the overseer of…Ankhefendjehuty, called …Nefer[ib]rasonb.'[206]

The caption above appears to read: 'Tomb of the fragile block in (…?) of upper end of court'.

204 I am indebted to E. Pischikova for this personal communication of 3. 11. 2010. TT 390 is on p. 440 in the *Top. Bibl.* erroneously said to be located at Assasif. Kampp, *Die thebanische Nekropole*, p. 620.

205 D. Eigner, *Die monumentalen Grabbauten der Spätzeit in der thebanischen Nekropole,* 1984.

206 I am indebted to Rune Nyord for attempting to disentangle this text.

Appendix I

Fragments of painted decoration from known Ramessid tombs

Most fragments of painted wall-decoration in museums and other collections stem from private tombs of the 18th dynasty, for which the reader is referred to Appendices I-III in Manniche, *Lost Tombs,* 1988. Some are, however, of Ramessid date, the majority remaining unidentified. A list of those known to the present writer is included here. TT 2, 215, 217, 218, 292 and 359 are at Deir el-Medina. TT 22 is opposite, at Gurnet Muraᶜi, whereas TT 113 is at Sheikh ᶜabd el-Qurna and TT 289 at Draᶜ abu el-Nagaᶜ. Basic pre-1960 bibliography for the tombs can be found in *Top. Bibl.*I,1.

TT 2

KHAᶜBEKHNET Servant in the Place of Truth. Temp. Ramesses II

1) This well known tomb at Deir el-Medina was visited first by Wilkinson, Hay and Burton, then by Lepsius who extracted a large portion of painted wall-decoration showing the tomb-owner offering to rows of kings, queens and princes. This now has Berlin no. 1625: *Top. Bibl.* I^2,1, p. 7 (10), cf. *Ausführliches Verzeichnis*, pp. 155-6. *In situ:* Lepsius, *Denkmäler*iii.2[a].

TT 113

KYNEBU wab-priest over-the-secrets of the estate of Amun, prophet in the Temple of Tuthmosis IV. Temp. Ramesses VIII

The monument was seen by Wilkinson, and also by Hay and his team, who made tracings and camera lucida drawings of the walls. The tomb was subsequently destroyed by a huge boulder rolling down from the cliff above. It can still be entered, though little remains on the walls (see Manniche, *City of the Dead*, 1988, pp. 110-1).

Three fragments of decorated mud plaster were presented to the British Museum by Hay's son in 1868.

1) BM 37993. Amenhotpe I, cf. *Top. Bibl.* I^2,1, p. 231 (2). To the references quoted there can be added T. G. H. James, *Egyptian Painting*, 1985, colour ill. 36.

2) BM 37994. Ahmosi Nefertere, cf. *Top. Bibl., loc. cit.*

3) BM 37995. Osiris, cf. *Top. Bibl, loc. cit.,* and James, *loc. cit.,* ill. 37.

TT 215 AMENEMOPET Royal scribe in the Place of Truth. 19th dyn.

This tomb was published by J. Jourdan, *Deux tombes de Deir el Medina. La tombe du scribe royal Amenemopet* (MIFAO lxxiii) Cairo 1939, pp. 25-46.

Based on the photographs published here, however, it is not possible to assign a specific place for these two fragments on the walls of the chapel, as indicated (but without argumentation) by M. Tosi in *Oriens Antiquus* 14, 1975, p. 139.

1) Museo Egizio, Turin no. prov. P. 776. H. 19 cm.
Tosi, pl. 29 (lower); G. Andreu and A.M. Donadoni Rover (eds), *Gli artisti del Faraone,* Milan 2003, cat. no. 226a (colour photo).

Face of a woman and part of a man's wig facing right. The woman wears a floral garland, unguent cone and lotus flower as well as a large earring. Hieroglyphs above the couple's heads mention the 'seat of eternity' and the end of a name the owner's name: *...ipt.* This would be the reason for an identification with TT215 (*sic* Andreu and Donadoni Roveri, as well as Tosi) whose owner has a similar name. According to Andreu and Donadoni Roveri, the fragment derives from the Drovetti collection (1824). But according to Jourdain, the first scholar engaged in work in TT 215 was Schiaparelli who excavated in Deir el-Medina in the early 1900's, and the fragments would seem seem more likely to have been picked up at this date. Typed cards from the museum has 'ancient stock' ('vecchio fondo').

2) Museo egizio, Turin, no. prov. P. 775, inv. no. 23614; h. 52cm.
Tosi, pl. 30; Andreu and Donadoni Roveri, cat. 226b.

Part of a vaulted ceiling showing a squatting deity in a scrine with a *kheker*-frieze on blueish-white background and a vertical band of text, with below part of a horizontal band of text and the upper extremity of the register below. On the left, hieroglyphs are painted on yellow, as are also those in the horizontal line below. Vertical columns of smaller hieroglyphs were sketched in red and corrected in black on blueish-white in the register below. The squatting deity is also painted on a blue background. The fragment may have belonged with the vignettes of the Book of Gates on the left wall of the vault of TT 215. The typed card in the museum has 'ancient stock', Andreu and Donadoni Roveri attributing it to Drovetti.

TT 217

IPUY  Sculptor. Ramesses II

The tomb, beautifully published by N. and N. de G. Davies in 1927,[207] was well known in the early 20th century, but it had already been entered in the early 1820s. A fragment from a wall was acquired by the museum in Berlin (no. 1104) from the collections of Baron Minutoli. Subsequently, during the years 1937-42, more fragments were cut out (see A. Fakhry 'A report on the inspectorate', 1946, pp. 31-4, one of them soon being identified by Keimer.

1) Berlin 1104 (fig. 65). Scribe and man plucking fowl, cf. *Top. Bibl.* I^2,1, p. 316 (5); W. Wreszinski, *Atlas zur ägyptischen Kulturgeschichte*, 1915, I, 385 [B] (*in situ* Davies, *Two Ramesside Tombs at Thebes,* 1927, pl. 30).

2) Man weighing meat, cf. *Top. Bibl.* I^2,1, p. 315 (2) and L. Keimer, 'Sur un monument égyptien du Musée du Louvre', in *RdE* 4, 1940, p. 62 (*in situ* Davies, pl. 38).

207 N. & N. de G. Davies, *Two Ramesside Tombs at Thebes*, 1927.

Fig. 65 Berlin 1104. (See p. 93).

Fig. 66 (drawn from photograph in auction catalogue)

TT 218

AMENNAKHT Servant in the Place of Truth on the West of Thebes. Ramessid

The earliest reference to this tomb is by Bruyère in the 1920's. A fragment appeared on the art market in 1979 (fig. 66):

1) Head of tomb-owner and wife, cf. *Top. Bibl.* I²,1, p. 317 (1): *Christie, Manson & Woods International Inc., Important Classical, Western, Arabic and Egyptian Antiquities sold on 25 January 1979,* no. 173; *id. 5 December 1979,* no. 266. The fragment, measuring 14.5 cm², was 'the property of an European collector'.

The provenance of the fragment was suggested in the auction catalogue. In view of the name of the tomb-owner and the unusual name of his wife (Iymway) as well as the style of the painting, this is convincing.

TT 222

HEKAMAETRA-NAKHT First Prophet of Monthu, Lord
called TURO of Thebes. Temp. Ramesses III-IV

This tomb has been known for some sixty years. It is now in a sorry state. At some stage the hall was burnt out, leaving just the tile-red mud plaster with faint outlines of figures. In the passage, which escaped the fire, countless small square pieces were cut out everywhere (cf. Manniche, *City of the Dead*, 1988, p. 68 with ill.) Some of these fragments have been identified, others are undoubtedly still on the art market.

1) Hildesheim, Pelizaeus-Museum 5262 (fig. 68). The fragment, showing the upper part of the tomb-owner and a column of hieroglyphs facing right, measures 33 x 21 cm. It was purchased by the museum in 1980, but had actu-

Fig. 67. Liverpool City Museum 26.22.543

Fig. 68 Pelizaeus-Museum 5262

ally been in the collection three or four years prior to this. The piece originally belonged on the left wall of the passage (*Top. Bibl.* I^2,1, pp. 323 (5) II).

2) Liverpool City Museum 56.22.543 (fig. 67). 54 x 45 cm. Fragment with man holding mummy, and female mourner, cf. *Top. Bibl.* I^2,1, pp. 323-4 (7); *National Museums & Galleries on Merseyside*, 2001 (cd).
The fragment was formally part of the Rustafjaell collection from which it was bought by a Dr. Fisher and presented to the Castle Museum, Norwich. In 1956 it was acquired by the Liverpool City Museum. The hieroglyphs on the fragment include the name of the tomb-owner.

3) Gallery Günther Puhze. Fragment measuring 23.5 x 28 cm showing a priest and a kite: *Kunst der Antike,* Katalog 4, 1982, no. 343, cf. N. M. Davies, 'An unusual depiction of Ramesside funerary rites', 1946, pl. XIII.

4) *Christie's, London, Sale* 16th *July 1985*, no. 181: upper part of person in panther skin with an inscription above (fig. 69).

Fig. 69

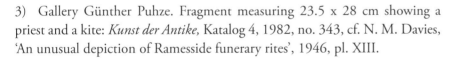

TT 286
NIAY Scribe of the table. Ramessid

The tomb was recorded by the Philadelphia University Museum, but it has not been published. Pieces were reported to have been removed from the tomb in the years 1937-42, but one was cut out at an earlier date, for in 1907 it came to the Louvre from the Cabinet de médailles. The original location of the fragment was probably in the hall ((3) II of *Top. Bibl.*)

1) Louvre E 13108: Row of relatives (*Top. Bibl.* I^2,1, p. 368 (3) II; see also A. Lhote & Hassia, *Chefs-d'oeuvres de la peinture égyptienne*, 1954, pl. 132; Manniche, *City of the Dead,* 1988, fig.68; C. Ziegler, *Le Louvre. Les antiquités égyptiennes*, 1990/1993, colour ill. on p. 54 (fig. 70).

Fig. 70 Louvre E 13108

TT 292

PESHEDU Servant in the Place of Truth. Temp. Sethos I-Ramesses II

Several tiny fragments from this tomb are now in the Museo egizio in Turin. In addition to reliefs from the court they include
Sup. no. 6150:

A) Seven fragments showing Ra-Harakhti, Harsiesi, and a man with child and offerings (*Top. Bibl.* I^2,1, p. 375 (9), cf. B. Bruyère, *Rapport sur les fouilles de Deir el Médineh (1923-1924),* p. 69, bottom (2°).

B) Parts of adoration of triads of Elephantine and Memphis (*Top. Bibl.* I^2,1, p. 375 (10), cf. Bruyère, *loc. cit.* (1 °)).

TT 359

INHERKHAꜥU Foreman of the Lord of the Two Lands in the Place of Truth. Temp. Ramesses III & IV.

In spite of the pillaging of the chapel, the burial chamber remains one of the most spectacular little tombs in the Theban necropolis. It was visited by Wilkinson and Lepsius, and it was finally published by Bruyère, *Rapport sur les fouilles de Deir el* Médineh (1930), pp. 32-70, 84-90.

The following pieces have been removed from the walls:

1) Ägyptisches Museum, Berlin no. 2026: Ahmosi Nefertere *Ägyptisches Museum* (1991), no. 89 with colour ill. (see also frontispiece).

2) Ägyptisches Museum, Berlin no. 2061: Amenhotpe I. *Ägyptisches Museum* (1991), no. 89 with colour ill.

Being about 160 cm tall, both these pieces are among the largest successfully removed from a tomb. They were acquired by Lepsius in 1845 and drawn by his expedition, presumably *in situ*, in his *Denkmäler* iii,1, cf. *Top. Bibl.* I,1, p. 422 (9) and (10).

3) British Museum EA 1291: Heads of a man and a woman facing left, T. G. H. James, *Egyptian Painting*, ill. 35.

4) British Museum EA 1329: Heads of tomb-owner and boy, James, *Egyptian Painting*, 1985, colour ill. 34.
5) British Museum EA 1291: Heads and shoulders of Inherkhau and his wife(?), T. G. H. James, *Egyptian Painting*, 1985, ill. 35.

For other fragments previously attributed to this tomb, see below, Appendix II.

Appendix II

Painted fragments of unknown provenance

As far as this was feasible, the fragments are grouped according to subject, but the headings should be taken with some caution, as in many cases the context remains conjectural.[208]

Deities

1) Ägyptisches Museum, (East) Berlin no. 18546 (figs. 71a-b); h 27 cm, w 21 cm. Formerly Rustafjaell collection. *Sotheby Sale Catalogue* 19-21 December 1906, no. 396[a]; *Top. Bibl.* I,1, p. 425; G. Roeder (ed.), *Aegyptische Inschriften* II, 1924, p. 171.
The fragment shows a seated king facing right with his name 'Lord of crowns, Amenhotpe, ruler of Thebes, given life'. It was suggested in the *Top. Bibl.* that the fragment might come from either TT 359 or TT 360. The former is an unlikely candidate, for the tomb already has two other representations of Amenhotpe I, one Berlin no. 2061, the other still *in situ* on the wall. There is no evidence of the subject having been depicted in TT 360.

Fig. 71 a-b Berlin 18546 and text from *Aegyptische Inschriften*

2) Philadelphia, University Museum E 14311;[209] h 54.7 cm. Purchased from Jos. Brumner 1925.
Painting on mud plaster showing a standing male deity facing left, with a kerchief in his left hand and an *ankh* in his right. To the right is a vertical border. The background is yellowish.

3) Formerly in the Rustafjaell collection; h 50.8 cm, w 53.8 cm. *Sotheby Sale Catalogue* 20-24 January 1913, no. 589 [a-c].
Three narrow upright panels each painted with a figure of a god holding the *ankh.* 'In fair preservation.'

4) Formerly in the Rustafjaell collection; h 35.5 cm, w. 25.4 cm. *Sotheby Sale Catalogue* 20-24 January 1913, no. 598[b].
Painted fragment with bright colouring showing a Hathor cow and small figures of men beneath.

5) *Christie's, London, Sale Catalogue 16 July 1985*, no. 185; h 25.4 cm, w 23.5 cm.
Painting on mud and gypsum showing a recumbent jackal and *udjat*-eye.

Fig. 72 Berlin 18548

6) Ägyptisches Museum, Berlin no. 18548 (fig. 72); w 10.5 cm.
Fragment showing head and chest of a bird-headed deity facing right.

208 Some of the fragments in the Museo egizio in Turin are very small and do not have separate inventory numbers. Many derive from the excavations of Schiaparelli early in the 20th century. Only the most significant pieces have been included here.
209 Seen by the author in 1982.

Men offering or adoring

7) City Museum and Art Gallery, Birmingham N 4072 (fig. 73); 29 x 6 cm; 13 x 8 cm.
Two fragments of painted limestone, one showing a person's bent arm, the other with part of a text on yellow background, mentioning 'Ptah, Lord of Truth': ...
The fragment on the right is no doubt the same piece as that from the Rustafjaell collection, *Sotheby Sale Catalogue* 9-10 December 1907, no. 163[b] 'fragment with an inscription'.

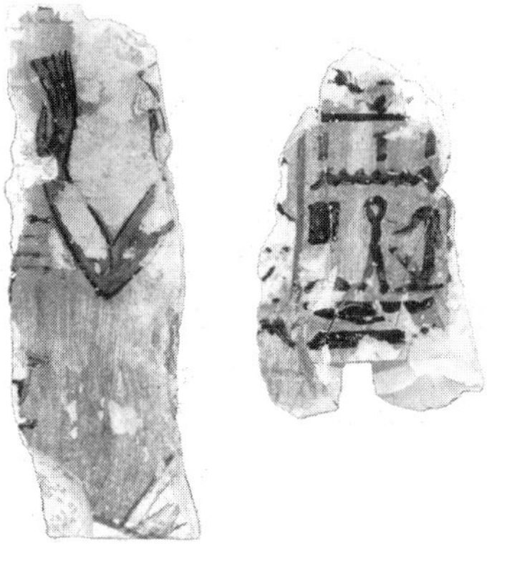

Fig. 73 Birmingham N 4072

8) Ägyptisches Museum, Berlin no. 1619 (fig. 74a-b); h. 42 cm.
Top. Bibl. I,1, p. 425; *LD Text* iii, p. 301 [middle]; *Ausführliches Verzeichnis,* 1899, p. 156; G. Roeder, *Aegyptische Inschriften* II, 1924, p. 171; GI Archive photo 42.
Head and shoulders of a man facing right *(sic)!* with arms raised in adoration, and surrounding hieroglyphic text. The background for this latter is white, the rest yellow. L. 2-7 of the text have been identified as being chapter 15 of the Book of the Dead.[210]
It is suggested in the *Top. Bibl.* that this fragment, together with two others, may come from TT 359 or TT 360. Lepsius first mentioned no. 1619 as coming from TT 359, as did the other two large pieces from TT 359 which he brought to Berlin: 'Aus diesem Grabe ist ein Wandfragment mit dem Kopf eines Mannes ... jetz Berlin 1619' (*Text* iii, p. 301). In the *Ausführliches Verzeichnis* of 1899 the piece is described as 'Kopf des Anhor-chaui... aus seimem Grabe' (p. 156). Here the height of the fragment is given as 52 cm. In the *Ägyptische Inschriften* published a few years later, Roeder copied the text, but indicates with an arrow that the person is facing left. This error is repeated by Bruyère in *Rapport sur les fouilles de Deir el Médineh (1939)*, p. 70. This scholar could find no room for the piece in TT 359, and hence he suggested the neighbouring TT 360. The columns dividing the hieroglyphs are still flanked by the first sketched lines marking the extent to which the signs could spread sideways. There is no trace of such lines in the decoration of TT 359. In TT 360, according to Bruyère, *op. cit.*, p. 82, the painting in this tomb is done directly on mud plaster. The fragment shows a white base coating.

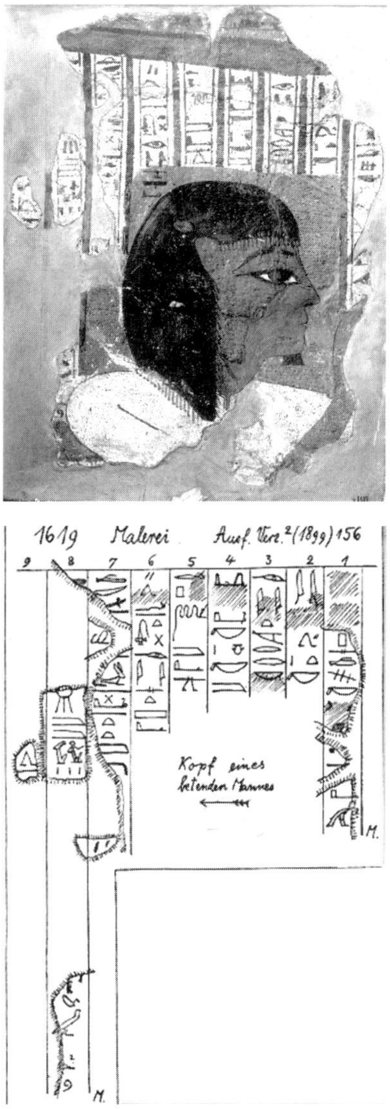

Fig. 74a-b Berlin 1619 and inscription from Roeder, *Ägyptische Inschriften*, II, 1924

9) *Christie's, London. Fine Antiquities* Wednesday 11 July 1984, no. 162; h 28 cm, w 20.3 cm.
Upper part of a man facing right. His right arm is raised in adoration, as was presumably his left.
He wears a white, sleeved tunic and a broad collar as well as a shoulder-length wig. The painting was done on mud plaster. On the photograph the background appears to be white.

10) *Galerie Günther Puhze. Katalog 1981. Kunst der Antike,* no. 316: h 28 cm, w 23 cm.
Painting on mud plaster with straw and a thin layer of stucco showing the upper part of a male figure facing right, with a double border line above and traces of hieroglyphs. His right arm is bent to the chest and the right, only visible from shoulder to elbow, reaches forward. The person wears a broad collar.

210 I owe this identification to Rune Nyord. A parallel can be found in I. Munro, *Der Totenbuch-Papyrus des Hohenpriesters Pa-nedjem II,* 1996, pl. 25, l. 14-15.

11) *Galerie Günther Puhze. Katalog 1981. Kunst der Antike,* no. 318; h. 28 cm, w 17 cm.
Painting on mud plaster and stucco with the upper part of a man, facing right, with one arm raised and wearing a white kilt. Colours well preserved. Slightly restored. The sales catalogue did not include a photograph of this fragment.

Fig. 75 Turin Suppl. 1349

12) Formerly in the Rustafjaell collection; 43.2 cm x 30.5 cm.
Sotheby Sales Catalogue 20-24 January 1913, no. 595.
The mud plaster fragment shows the upper part of a figure draped in a 'leopard's skin' (probably the panther skin of a *sem* priest) over which is a broad band embroidered with the names and titles of a king Ramesses. The person holds an incense burner. According to the sales catalogue, this fragment was 'well painted and rare'.

13) Turin Suppl. 1349 (this number includes 6 other pieces) (fig. 75).
Acquired through Schiaparelli 1900-01.
Man facing right, a staff in his left hand, a sceptre and *ankh*-sign in his right. He wears a double kilt, tunic and collar. Lines are apparent on his belly through the fabric.

Fig. 76

14) *Sotheby's, New York* May 22, 1981, no. 40 (fig. 76).
Upper part of two male offering bearers facing right. They both carry a chest, and the foremost a vase(?). The background is white and apparently mud plaster. 20.3 x 28.5 cm.

Women offering or adoring

15) Ägyptisches Museum, Berlin no. 18552 (fig. 77); h 16 cm.
Formerly Rustafjaell collection, cf. *Sotheby Sale Catalogue* 19-21 December 1906, no. 399[c], pl. VIII,13.
Woman with long wig and unguent cone facing left and with her arms raised.

16) Formerly in the Rustafjaell collection.
Sotheby Sale Catalogue 9-10 December 1907, no. 157.
Woman with long wig, floral diadem and both arms raised, facing right.

17) Hermitage, Leningrad inv. no. 8735; h 24.5 cm, w. 17.7 cm.
Egyptian Art in the Hermitage, no. 40
Painted limestone with upper part of a woman facing right with both arms raised. Very summary representation. Outlines restored?

18) Formerly in the Rustafjaell collection.
Sotheby Sale Catalogue 19-21 December 1906, no. 395[b]
Woman with a long wig facing right, holding a stem of papyrus in her left arm, which has a bracelet. According to a marked copy of the sale catalogue, the fragment was 'sold to Llewellyn'.

Fig. 77 Berlin 18552

19) *Galerie Günther Puhze. Katalog 1981. Kunst der Antike,* no. 319; h 40 cm, w 25 cm.
Painting on stucco depicting a woman with offerings, facing right.

Fig. 78

'Banquet scenes'

As mentioned above, p. 74, this subject was a very popular one among those removing fragments from tombs. With the close of the 18th dynasty, it became far less frequently depicted, but the rows of elaborately dressed men and women are reflected in depictions of 'relatives' in Ramessid tombs. Included under this heading are in the present place also fragments of the tomb-owner and/or his wife who may have been the recipents of offerings.

20) *Christie's, London, Antiquities and Primitive Art,* 5 December 1977, no. 67; h 33.7 cm, w 25.4 cm.
Painted plaster with a scene showing man and wife seated upon a couch before a laden offering table. The man wears a shoulder-length wig, short beard, white collar and kilt and holds a lotus flower. His wife has her arm around his shoulder and wears a wig, collar and pleated skirt. A 20th dynasty date was suggested.

Fig. 79 Louvre E 13009

21) Formerly in the Rustafjaell collection.
Sotheby Sale Catalogue 9-10 December 1907, no. 159[b], pl. IV [right]
A fragment showing a representation of the upper half of a man and the face of a woman, turned towards the left. An arm and lotus flower have been awkwardly restored. A border is visible along the upper edge.

22) Formerly Sir Sidney Nolan collection (UK) (fig. 78). Postcard from Rupert Wace Ancient Art, London.
Head of a man facing right, wearing a broad necklace and sniffing a lotus flower. Yellow background.

23) Formerly in the Rustafjaell collection.
Sotheby Sale Catalogue 9-10 December 1907, no. 159[a], pl. IV [left].
Head of a man, facing right, with an unguent cone and a band tied around it. A few hieroglyphs remain before his face:  .

24) Louvre, Paris E 13099 (Cabinet des médailles no. 84) (fig. 79 upper); h 35.1 cm, w 29.1 cm.
La vie au bord du Nil au temps des pharaons (Exhibition catalogue Calais, cat. no. 3; *Naissance de l'écriture,* no. 94 (text).
Painted plaster with seated lady with a lotus flower facing left (legs missing). The piece was formerly displayed with a horizontal piece of text, perhaps from elsewhere.

Fig. 80 Turin

25) Museo egizio, Turin (fig. 80).
Face of a woman, turned towards the left, with a large earring.

26) Museo egizio, Turin (fig. 81).
Face of a woman, turned towards the right.

Funerary subjects

27) Museo egizio, Turin, inv. no. 23616; h 17 cm, w 21 cm.
Fragment of mud mixed with straw and coated with stucco, showing a ba-bird on a shrine, facing right, on white background, probably from the same tomb as no. 26.

Fig. 81 Turin

28) Museo egizio, Turin inv. no.15993 (fig. 82).
Seven fragments depicting the fields of the blessed on a blueish-white background. The tallest fragment, covering two registers with bordering strips, measures 26 cm in height. Two strips of water divide the scene into three registers, the lower one being a floral border. The middle register shows ploughing and harvesting. To the left in the upper register are two squatting figures facing left towards an offering table and two male figures in long white garments. To the right are fragments of lakes. The fragments are painted on mud plaster mixed with straw and a thin layer of plaster. They were acquired by Schiaparelli in 1900-01.

Fig. 82 Turin

29) Museo egizio, Turin (fig. 83).
Upper part of a woman receiving libation from a tree goddess. Between them are three loaves.

Fig. 83 Turin

30) Ägyptisches Museum, Berlin no. 18545 (fig. 84).
Formerly Rustafjaell collection, *Sotheby Sale Catalogue* 19-21 December 1906, no. 400[b], pl. VIII,14; cf. *Top. Bibl.* I^2,1, p. 425; text: G. Roeder, *Aegyptische Inschriften* II, 1924, p. 170.
Fragment of mud plaster mixed with straw with painting on dark blue background,[211] showing the upper part of a man with two jets of water coming down on either side of his body. He has a floral collar around his neck. Parts of seven columns of hieroglyphs remain above. These are taken from chapter 110 of the Book of the Dead with gaps. Compared with the Book of the Dead of Juja ll. 1 and 2 correspond to col. 550, ll. 3-4 to col. 551 and l. 5 to ll. 551-2, while ll. 6 and 7 correspond to col 554 and 556.[212]
It is suggested in the *Top. Bibl.* that the fragment comes from TT 359 or 360. As it is painted on a layer of stucco it cannot come from TT 360, where the decoration is applied directly on the mud plaster. The dividing columns have the same guide lines as fragment no. 8, which are non existent in TT 359, hence this is an equally unlikely candidate. The piece comes from the Rustafjaell collection, and there is nothing in particular to connect it with Deir el-Medina. In fact, one may ask if the fragment would not be more at home in the 18th dynasty than in the Ramessid period.

Fig. 84 Berlin 18545 and text from G. Roeder, *Ägyptische Inschriften* II, p. 170

211 Notes taken by the author in 1975.
212 I am indebted to Rune Nyord for these references. For the parallels cf. I. Munro, *Die Totenbuch-Handschriften der 18. Dynastie*, 1994 II, pl. 60, col. 550-556.

31) Liverpool City Museum M 14056. H. 20 cm, w. 18 cm.
C. Gatty, *Catalogue of the Mayer Collection I*, 1879, p. 57, no. 365; P. Bienkowski and A. Tooley, *Gifts of the Nile*, 1995, p. 60, pl. 92; *National Museums & Galleries on Merseyside*, 2001 (cd).
The fragment shows a kneeling man, facing right, receiving jets of water, presumably from a tree goddess. The background is white. It was part of the Joseph Mayer Collection and was presented to the museum in 1867.

Other subjects

Fig. 85 Turin 1341

32) Museo egizio, Turin suppl. no. : 1341 (sic museum photo - in the *Top. Bibl.* fragments of an 18th dynasty music scene are listed under this number) (fig. 86). H 16 cm, w 20 cm.
E. Scamuzzi, *Museo egizio... Guida* [1965], pp. 26-7.
Head of a woman, facing left, and upper part of a boy with boomerang and bird. The boy has a white necklace and white earring.

33) Museo egizio, Turin prov. no. 778 (fig. 86).
Seated woman facing left holding three fishes. In front of her two hieroglyphs  which may be part of her name (Mutemwiya?).
The subject would be at home in TT 217, except for the fact that the scenes here take place at the river bank,[213] not where one would expect to find a chair.

Fig. 86 Turin excav. no. 778

34) Museo egizio inv. nos. 23731, 23733-6.
Several small fragments of floral borders or similar, some from Schiaparelli excavations 1905 at Deir el-Medina.

213 Cf. N. de G. Davies, *Two Ramesside Tombs at Thebes*, 1927, pl. XL,3. The style is somewhat reminiscent of that found in TT 178, where the wife is in fact called Mutemwia. But one would hardly find the occupant of the tomb as a fishmonger.

Bibliography and Indices

Bibliographical abbreviations

AO	*Acta Orientalia,* Copenhagen
ASAE	*Annales du Service des antiquités,* Cairo
CdE	*Chronique d'Égypte,* Brussels
GM	*Göttinger Miszellen,* Göttingen
JARCE	*Journal of the American Research Center in Cairo,* Cairo
JEA	*Journal of Egyptian Archaeology,* London
LdÄ	*Lexikon der Ägyptologie,* Wiesbaden 1972-92
MÄS	*Münchener ägyptologische Studien,* Munich
MDAIK	*Mitteilungen des deutschen archäologischen Instituts Kairo,* Mainz
OMRO	*Oudhedkundige Mededeelingen uit's Rijksmuseum van Oudheden te Leiden,* Leiden
Papyrus	*Magazine of the Danish Egyptological Society,* Copenhagen
RdE	*Revue d'Égyptologie,* Paris
SAGA	*Studien zur Archäologie und Geschichte Altägyptens,* Heidelberg
ZÄS	*Zeitschrift für ägyptische Sprache,* Leipzig

K*RI* see Kitchen
Top. Bibl. see Porter and Moss

Bibliography

Works abbreviated in the text:

Assmann, J., 'Helligt rum i ramessidiske privatgrave, *Papyrus* 20/2, 2000, pp. 3-10.

Aston, D. A., 'An enigmatic cartouche', *GM* 106, 1988, pp. 15-19.

Aston, D. A., (Review of A. Niwinski, 21st Dynasty Coffins from Thebes), *JARCE* 28, 1992, pp. 233-4.

Aston, D. A., 'The Shabti Box: A Typological Study', *OMRO* 74, Leiden 1994, pp. 21-54.

Aston, D. A., 'Psusennes II and Shoshenq I', *JEA* 79, 1993, pp. 267-8.

Ausführliches Verzeichnis der aegyptischen Altertümer und Gipsabgüsse. Königliche Museen zu Berlin, 1899.

Bács, T. A., 'First preliminary report on the work of the Hungarian mission in Thebes in Theban Tomb No. 65 (Nebamun/Imiseba)', *MDAIK* 54, 1998, pp. 49-64.

Barthelmess, P., *Die Übergang ins Jenseits in den thebanischen Beamtengräbern der Ramessidenzeit* (SAGA 2), Heidelberg 1992.

Bell, L., 'Return to Dra Abu el Naga', *Expedition* 11/3, Spring 1969, pp. 26-37.

Bienkowski, P. and A. Tooley, *Gifts of the Nile*, Liverpool 1995.

Binder, S., *The Gold of Honour in New Kingdom Egypt*, Oxford 2008.

Borchardt, L., 'Die Königin bei einer feierlichen Staatshandlung Ramses' II', *ZÄS* 67, 1931, pp. 29-31, pls. I, II.

Borghouts, J. F., *Book of the Dead (39). From Shouting to Structure*, Wiesbaden 2007.

Brockhuis, J., *De godin Renenwetet*, Assen 1971.

Bruyère, B., *Mert Seger à Deir el Médineh*, Cairo 1929.

Bruyère, B., *Rapport sur les fouilles de Deir el Médineh*, Cairo 1924-53.

Boreux, C., *Guide-catalogue sommaire*, Paris 1932.

Burkard, G., M. Mackensen, and D. Polz, 'Die spätantike/koptische Klosteranlage Deir el-Bachit in Dra' Abu el-Naga (Oberägypten). Erster Vorbericht', *MDAIK* 59, 2003, pp. 41-65.

Capart, J., 'Quelques figurines funeraires d'Amenemopet', *CdE* 15, 1940, pp. 190-6.

Champollion, J. F., *Monuments de l'Égypte et de la Nubie*, I-IV, 1835-45.

Champollion, J. F., *Notices descriptives conformes aux notices autographes rédigées sur les lieux par Champ. le jeune*, I-II, 1844-89.

Davies, N. de G., *Two Ramesside Tombs at Thebes*, New York 1927.

Davies, N. M., 'An unusual depiction of Ramesside funerary rites', *JEA* 32, 1946, pp. 69-70.

Dawson, W. R. and E. Uphill, *Who was Who in Egyptology*, 3rd ed., London 1995.

de Buck, A., *The Egyptian Coffin Texts*, Chicago 1918.

Eichner, I. and U. Fauerbach, 'Die spätantike/koptische Klosteranalge Deir el-Bachit in Draᶜ Abu el-Naga (Oberägypten). Zweiter Vorbericht', *MDAIK* 61, 2005, pp. 139-152.

Eigner, D., *Die monumentalen Grabbauten der Spätzeit in der thebanischen Nekropole*, Vienna 1984.

Fakhry, A., 'A Report on the Inspectorate of Upper Egypt', *ASAE* 46, 1946, pp. 25-54.

Faulkner, R. O., *The Ancient Egyptian Book of the Dead*, London 1985.

Fecht, G., 'Schicksalgöttinnen und König', *ZÄS* 105, 1978, pp. 14-42.

Fischer, H. G., *L'écriture et l'art de l'Egypte ancienne*, Paris 1986.

Gaballa, G.A. and K. A. Kitchen, 'The festival of Sokar', *Orientalia* 38, 1969, pp. 1-78.

Gatty, C., *Catalogue of the Mayer Collection I*, London 1879.

Golenischev, W., *Ermitage Imperial. Inventaire de la collection égyptienne*, 1891.

Graindorge, C., 'Les oignons de Sokar', *RdÉ* 43, 1982, pp. 87-105.

Helck, W., *Materialien zur Wirtschaftsgeschichte des Neuen Reiches*, Wiesbaden 1960.

Hofman, E., *Das Grab des Neferronpet gen. Kenro (TT 178)*, Mainz 1995.

Hölscher, U., *The Excavation of Medinet Habu*, iii, Chicago 1941.

James, T. G. H., *Egyptian Painting*, London 1985.

Jansen-Winkeln, K., *Inschriften der Spätzeit* I-II, Wiesbaden 2007.

Janssen, J. J., *Nine Letters from the Times of Ramses II*, OMRO 41, Leiden 1960.

Jaritz, H. *et al.*, 'Der Totentempel des Merenptah in Qurna. 1. Grabungsbericht (1.-6. Kampagne)' *MDAIK* 48, 1992, pp. 65-91; 'Der Totentempel des Merenptah in Qurna. 2. Grabungsbericht (7.und 8. Kampagne)', *MDAIK* 51, 1995, pp. 57-83; 'Der Totentempel des Merenptah in Qurna. 3. Grabungsbericht (9. und 10. Kampagne),' *MDAIK* 52, 1996, pp. 201-232; 'Der Totentempel des Merenptah in Qurna. 5. Grabungsbericht', *MDAIK* 57, 2001, pp. 141-170.

Jørgensen, M., *Catalogue Egypt II (1550-1080 B.C.)*, Copenhagen 2001.

Kampp, F., *Die thebanische Nekropole* I-II, Mainz am Rhein 1996.

Keimer, L., 'Sur un monument égyptien du Musée du Louvre', *RdE* 4, 1940, pp. 45-65.

Kikuchi, T., 'Die thebanische Nekropole der 21. Dynastie: Zum Wandel der Nekropole und zum Totenglauben der Ägypter', *MDAIK* 58, 2002, pp. 343-371.

Kitchen, K., *Ramesside Inscriptions*, Oxford 1975-2003.

Kitchen, K., *The Third Intermediate Period*, Warminster 1973.

Lapp, G., *Totenbuch Spruch 17*, Totenbuchtexte 1, Basel 2006.

Leitz, C., *Lexikon der ägyptischen Götter und Götterbezeichnungen*, (OLA 110-117), Leiden 2002.

Lepsius, K. R., *Denkmäler aus Aegypten und Aethiopien*, I-XII, 1849-59 with *Text* vols.

Lhote, A. and Hassia, *Chefs-d'oeuvres de la peinture égyptienne*, Paris 1954.

Lucarelli, R., 'The vignette of ch. 40 of the Book of the Dead', OLA 150, Louvain 2007 vol. 2, pp. 1181-6.

Lüddekens, E., 'Untersuchungen über religiösen Gehalt, Sprache und Form der ägyptischen Totenklagen', *MDAIK* 11, 1943, pp. 1-187.

Manniche, L., *An Ancient Egyptian Herbal,* London and Austin, Texas 1987, 2nd revised ed. 2006.

Manniche, L., *Ancient Egyptian Musical Instruments* (MÄS 34), Munich 1975.

Manniche, L. *City of the Dead. Thebes in Egypt,* London/ Chicago 19187; also published as *The Tombs of the Nobles at Luxor,* Cairo 1988.

Manniche, L., 'Forsvundne grave fra ramessidetiden', *Papyrus* 17/2, 1997, pp. 11-17.

Manniche, L., *Lost Tombs. A Study of Certain Eighteenth Dynasty Monuments in the Theban Necropolis,* London 1988.

Manniche, L., 'The complexion of queen Ahmosi Nefertere', *AO* 40, 1979, pp. 11-19.

Medinet Habu I-VIII, The University of Chicago Oriental Institute Publications, Chicago 1930-70.

Muhammed, Abdel-Qader, *The Development of the Funerary Beliefs and Practises in the Private Tombs of the New Kingdom at Thebes,* Cairo 1966.

Munro, I., *Totenbuch-Handschriften der 18. Dynastie im Ägyptischen Museum Cairo,* Wiesbaden 1994.

Munro, I., *Die Totenbuch-Handschriften der 18. Dynastie im Ägyptischen Museum Cairo,* Ägyptologische Abhandlungen 54, Wiesbaden 1994.

National Museums & Galleries on Merseyside. Liverpool, Egyptian Treasures in Europe, Utrecht 2001 (cd).

Naville, E., *Inscription historique de Pinodjem III,* Paris 1883.
Naville, E., *The XIth Dynasty Temple of Deir el-Bahari,* London 1907-13.

Newberry, P. E., 'Topographical notes on Western Thebes collected in 1830 by Joseph Bonomi', *ASAE* 7, 1906, p. 78-86.

Niwinski, A., *Studies on the illustrated Funerary Papyri of the 11th and 10th centuries B.C.,* Fribourg 1989.

Otto, E., *Topographie des thebanischen Gaues,* Berlin/Leipzig 1952.

Parkinson, R. B., *Cracking Codes,* London 1999.

Parkinson, R. B., *Reading Ancient Egyptian Poetry among other Histories,* Oxford 2009.

Pijoan, J., *Summa Artis. Historia general del arte Volume III. El arte egipcio,* Madrid 1950.

Porter, B. & Moss, R. L. B., *Topographical Bibliography of Ancient Egyptian Hieroglyphic Texts, Reliefs, and Paintings.* I *The Theban Necropolis.* Part 1 *Private Tombs,* Oxford 1960/1970; Part 2 *Royal Tombs and Smaller Cemeteries,* Oxford 1964/1973; II *Theban Temples,* Oxford 1972.

Radwan, A., *Darstellungen des regierenden Königs in den Beamtengräber der 18. Dynastie* (MÄS 21), Munich 1969.

Roeder, G. (ed.), *Aegyptische Inschriften aus den königlichen Museen zu Berlin,* I-II, Leipzig 1901-24.

Rößler-Köhler, U., *Kapitel 17 des ägyptischen Totenbuches,* (Göttinger Orientforschungen IV.10), Wiesbaden 1979.

Rosellini, I., *I monumenti dell'Egitto e della Nubia* I-III, Pisa 1832-44.

Saleh, M., *Darstellungen des Totengerichts in den thebanischen Beamtengräber des Neuen Reiches,* Mainz-am-Rhein 1984.

Scamuzzi, E., *Museo egizio di Torino. Guida allo statuario e alle sale del primo piano* (Booklet, no date, but prior to 1965).

Schneider, H. D., *Shabtis. An introduction to the history of Ancient Egyptian funerary statuettes with a catalogue of the collection of shabtis in the National Museum of Antiquities in Leiden,* Leiden 1977.

Schott, S., *Das schöne Fest vom Wüstentale,* Wiesbaden 1953.

Seeber, C., *Untersuchungen zur Darstellung des Totengerichts im Alten Ägypten* (MÄS 35), Munich 1976.

Sethe, K., 'Die Berufung eines Hohenpriesters des Amon unter Ramses II', *ZÄS* 44, 1907-8, pp. 30-5.

Strudwick, N. and J. H. Taylor (eds.), *The Theban Necropolis*, London 2003.

Thompson, J., *Sir Gardner Wilkinson and his Circle*, Austin, Texas 1992.

Tillet, S., *Egypt Itself*, London 1984.

van Walsem, R., *The Coffin of Djedmonthuiufankh in the National Museum of Antiquities at Leiden I-II*, Leiden 1997.

von Lieven, A., 'Kleine Beiträge zur Vergöttlichung Amenophis I' (1), *RdE* 51, 2000, pp. 103-21.

von Lieven, A., 'Kleine Beiträge zur Vergöttlichung Amenophis' I (2). Der Amenophis-Kult nach dem Ende des Neuen Reiches', *ZÄS* 128, 2001, pp. 41-64.

Wilkinson, J. G., *The Manners and Customs of the Ancient Egyptians* (ed. Birch), New York 1878.

Wreszinski, W., *Atlas zur ägyptischen Kulturgeschichte*, Leipzig 1915.

Ziegler, C., *Le Louvre. Les antiquités égyptiennes*, Paris 1990/1993.

Indices

Personal names (excluding Appendix I-II)

Titles (excluding Appendix I-II)

Special locations

Early travellers

Early tomb numbers

Champollion
no. 27 = TT C7
no. 28 = TT C6
no. 39 = TT A15
no. 40 = TT A12
Rosellini
no. 28 = TT C6
no. 27 = TT C7
no. 40 = TT A15
no. 41 = TT A12

Special subjects

List of illustrations